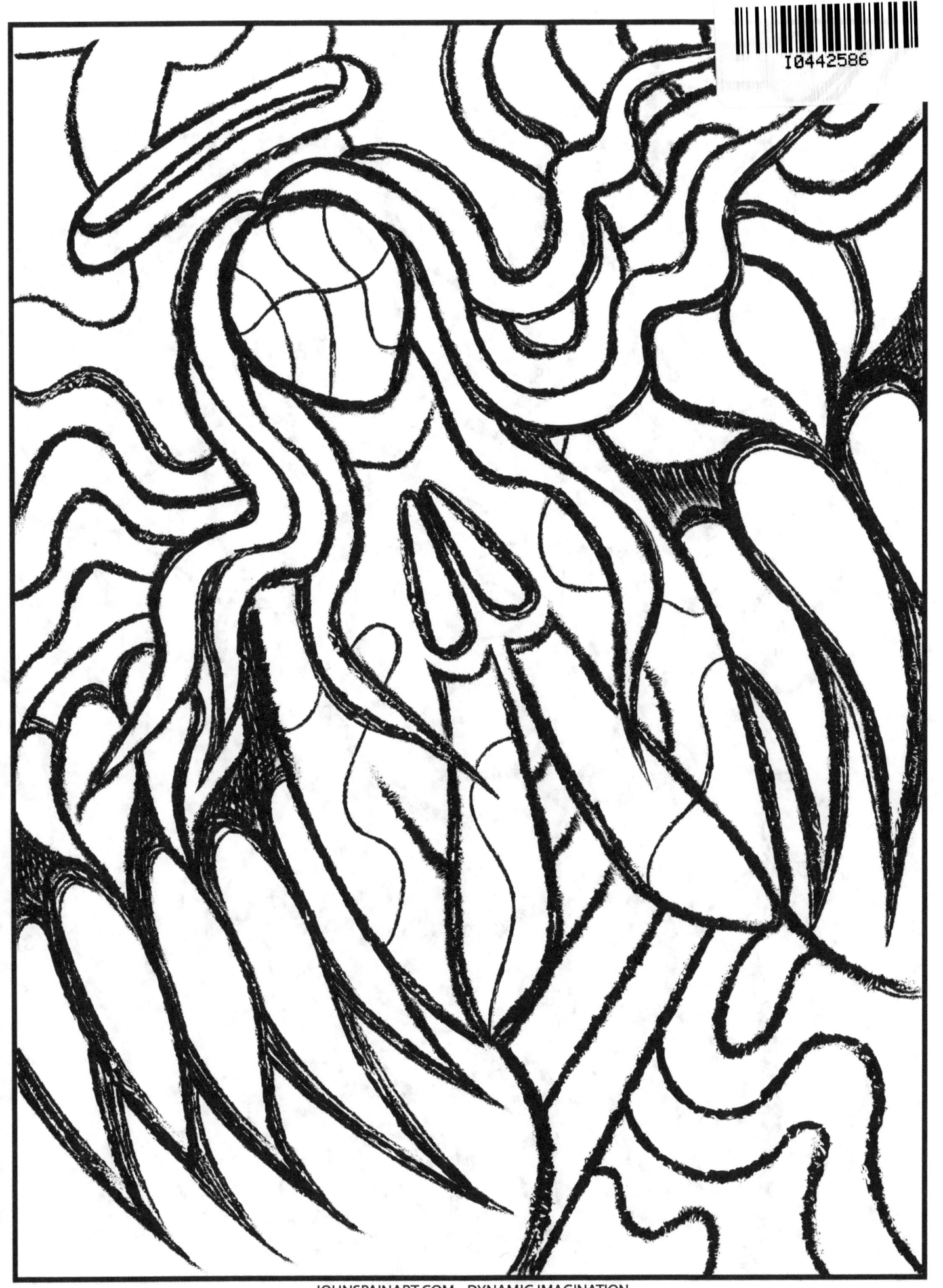

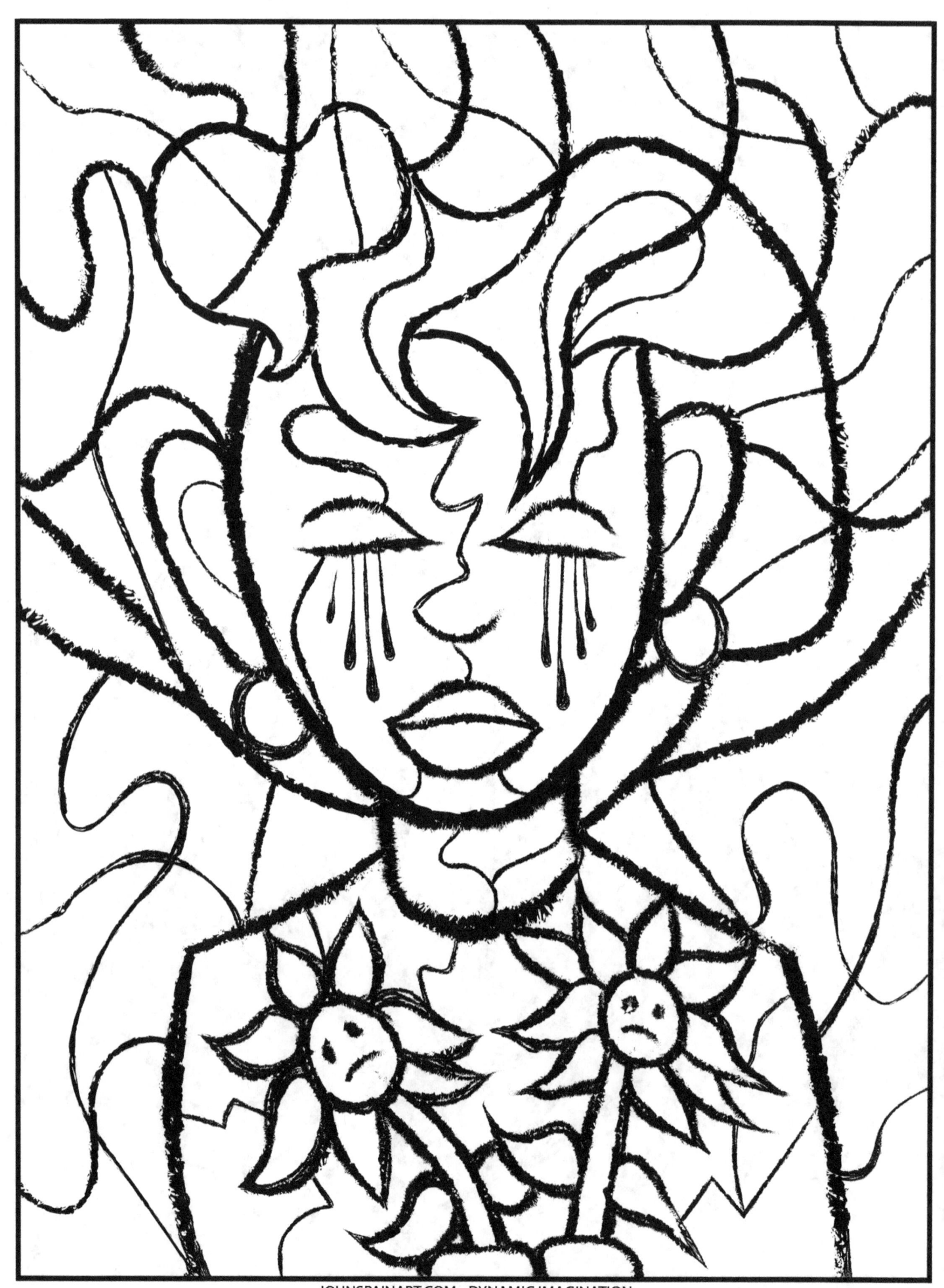

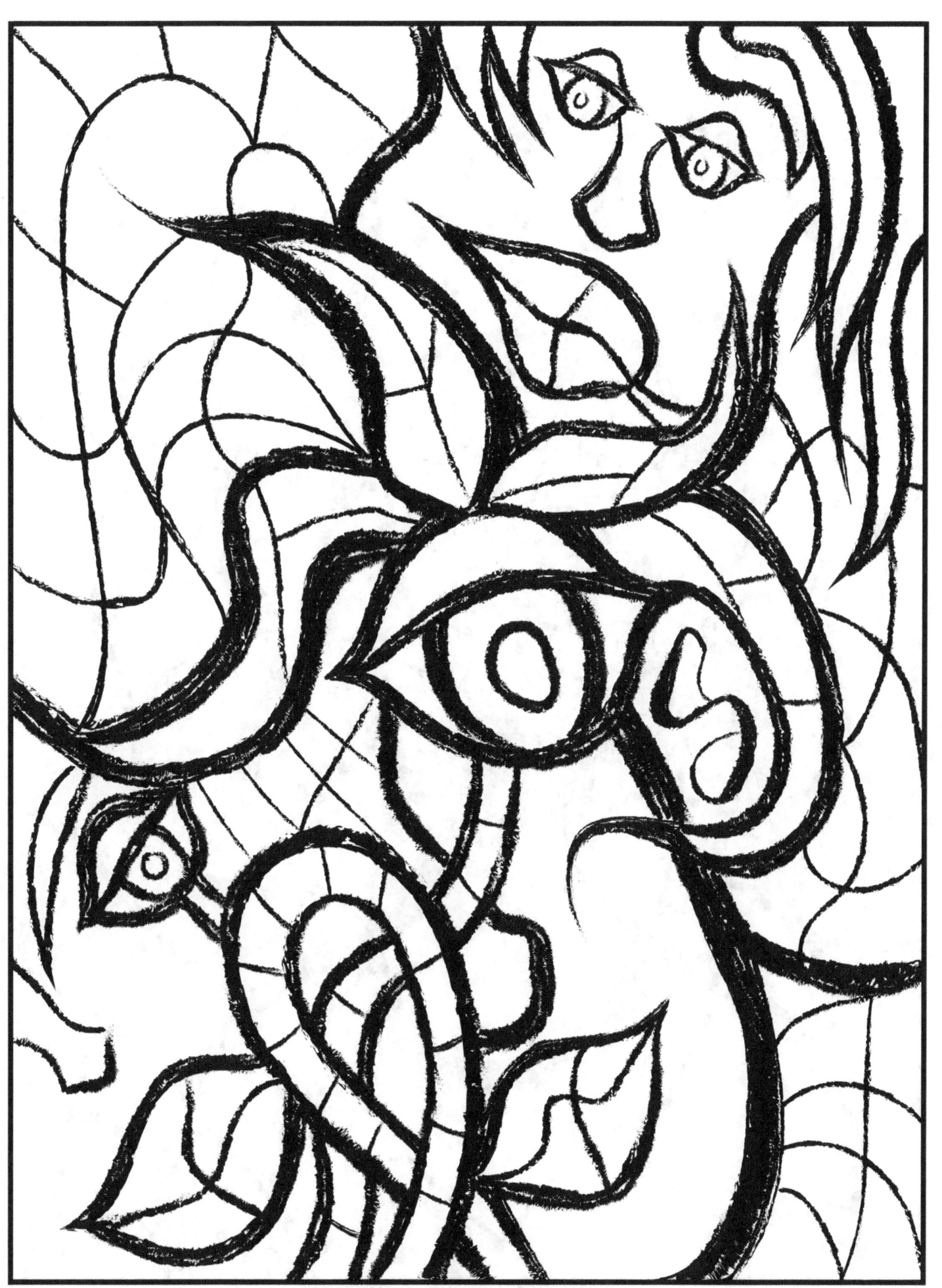

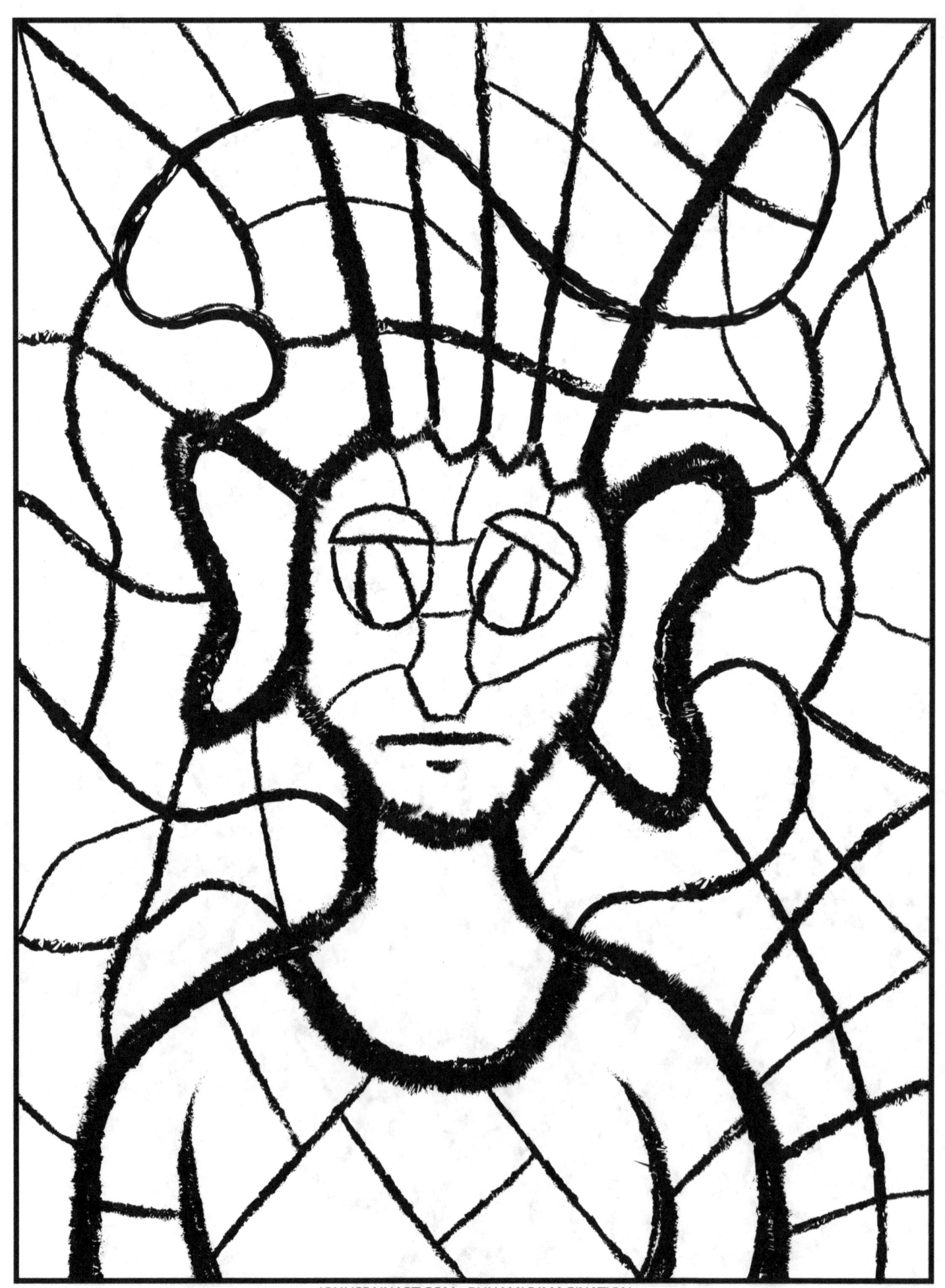

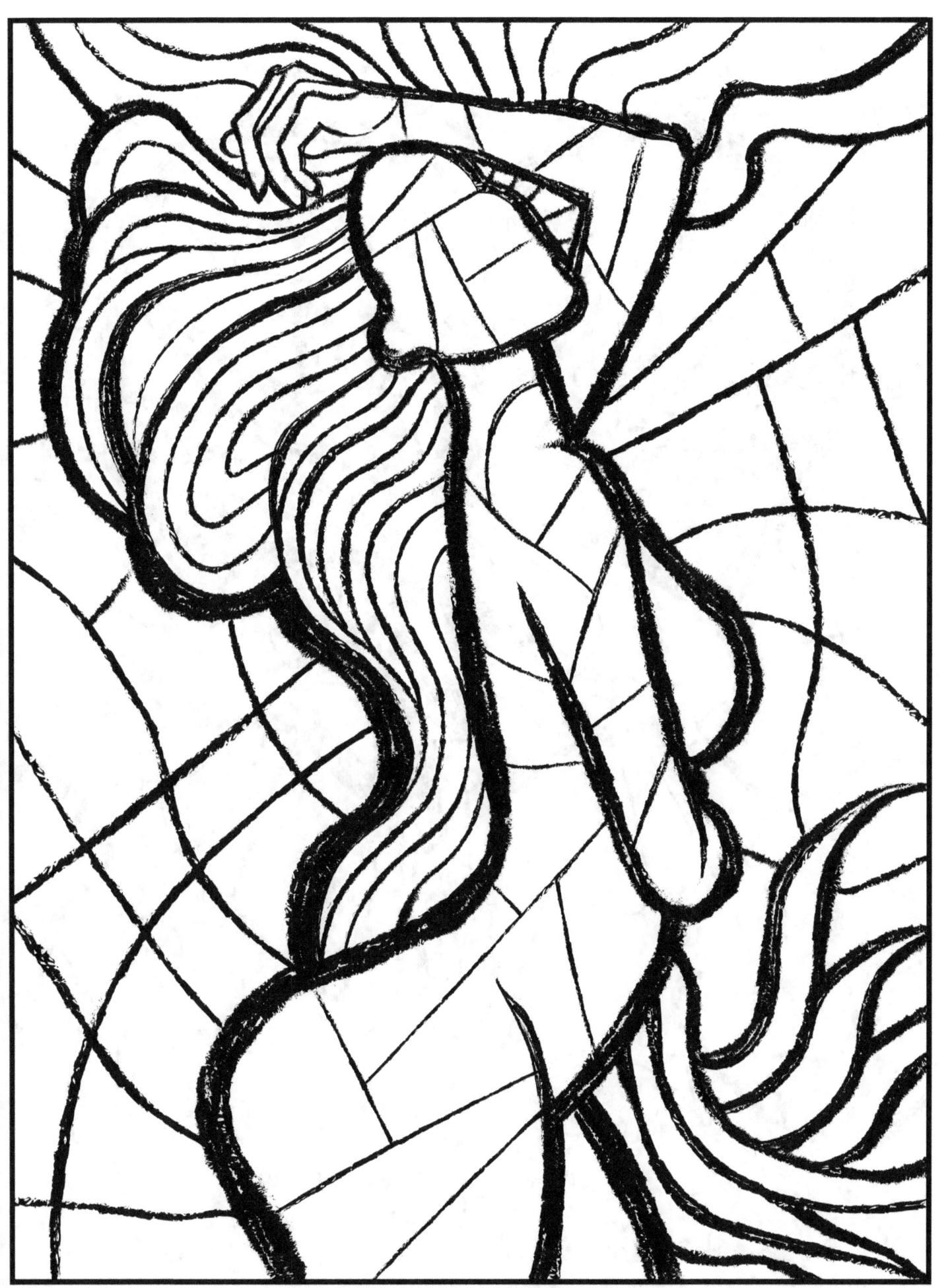

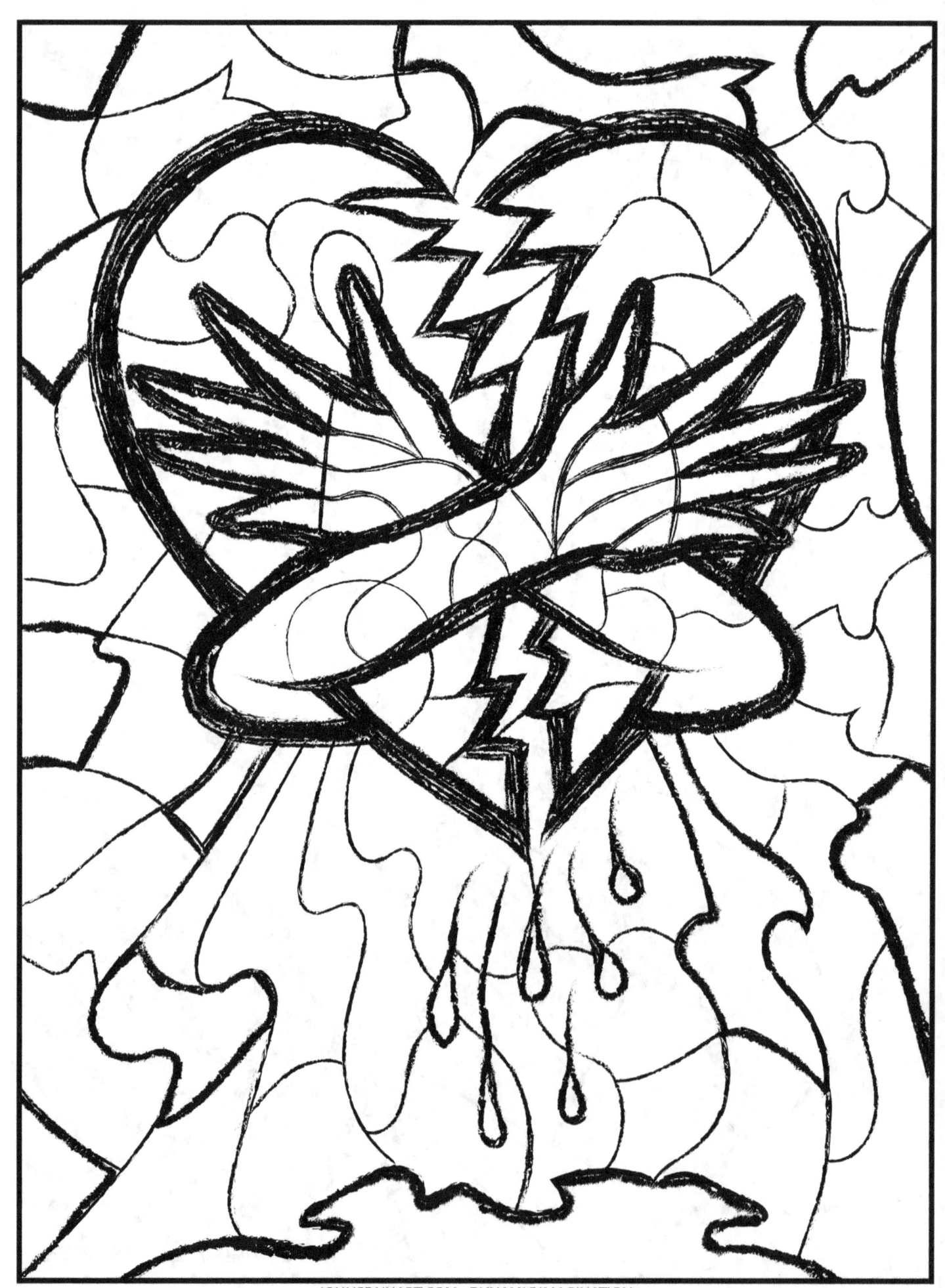

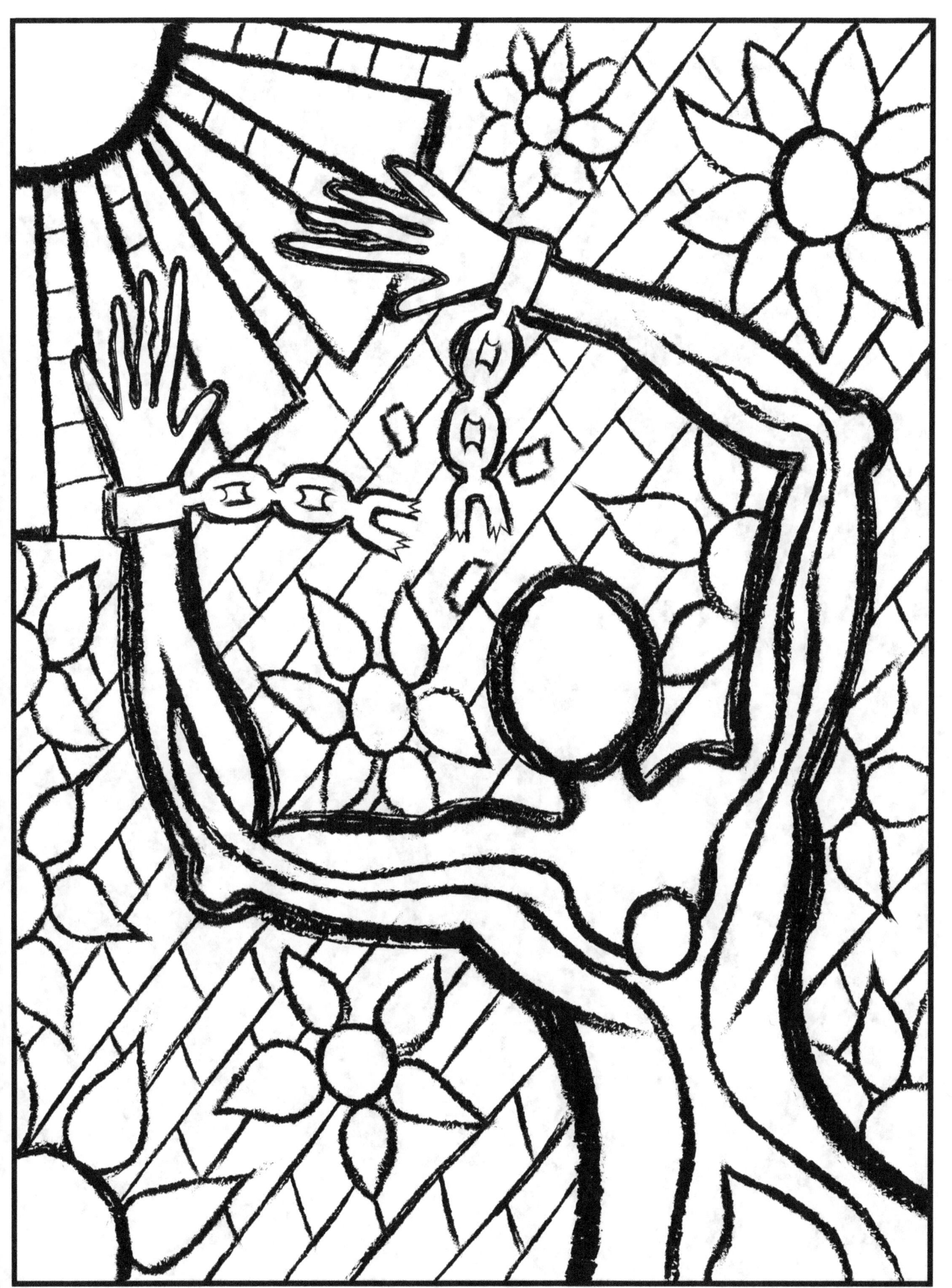

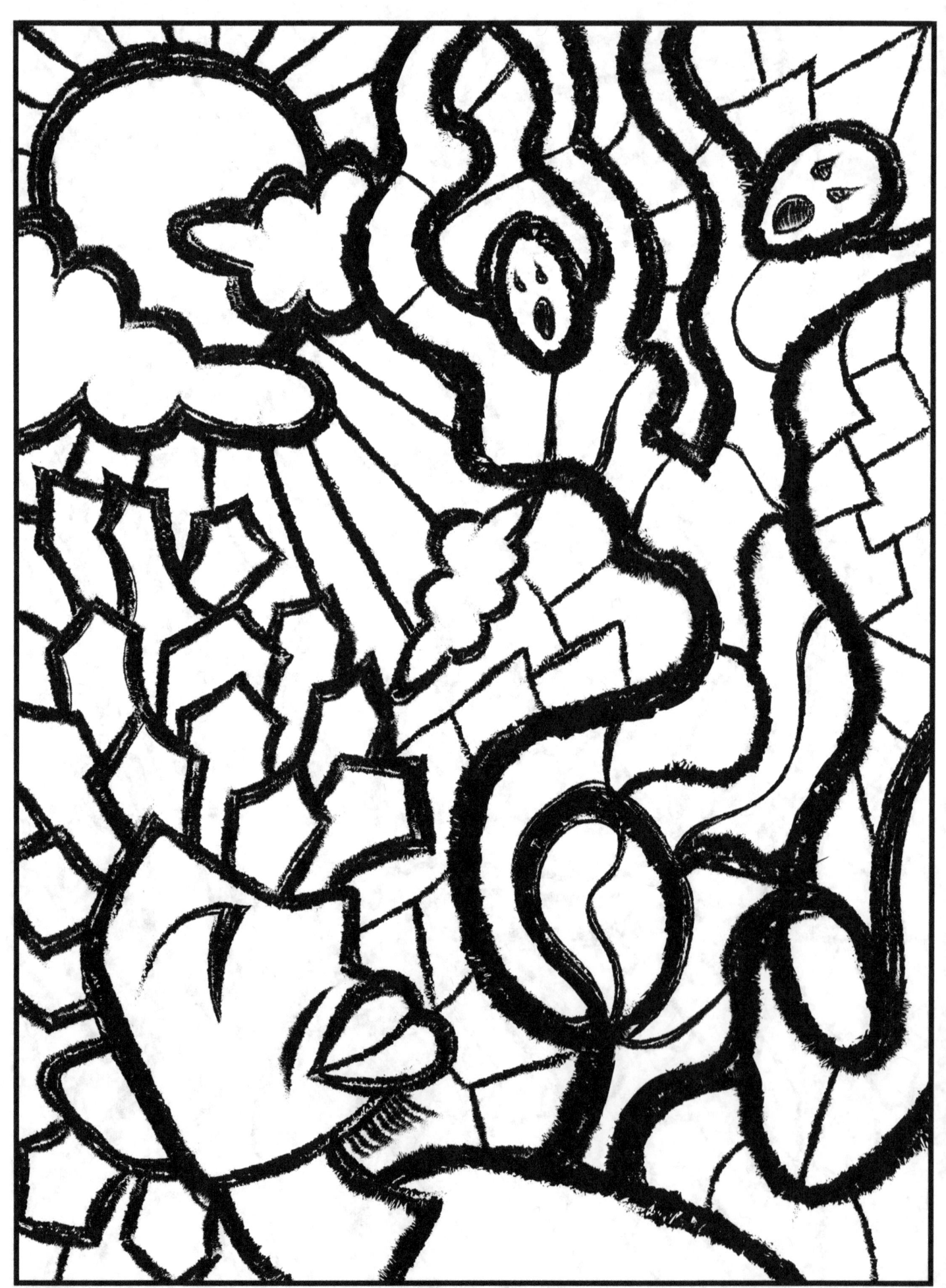

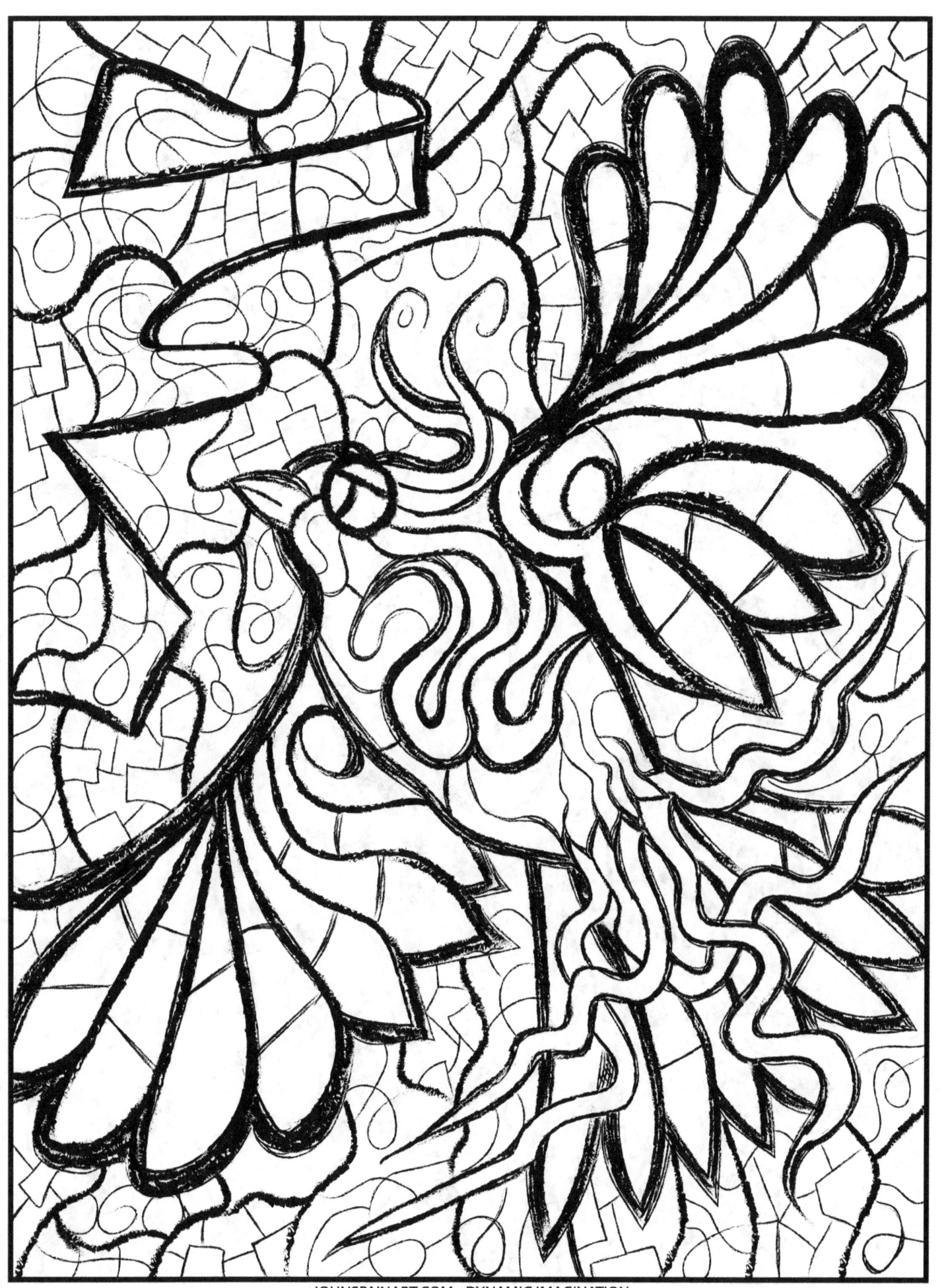

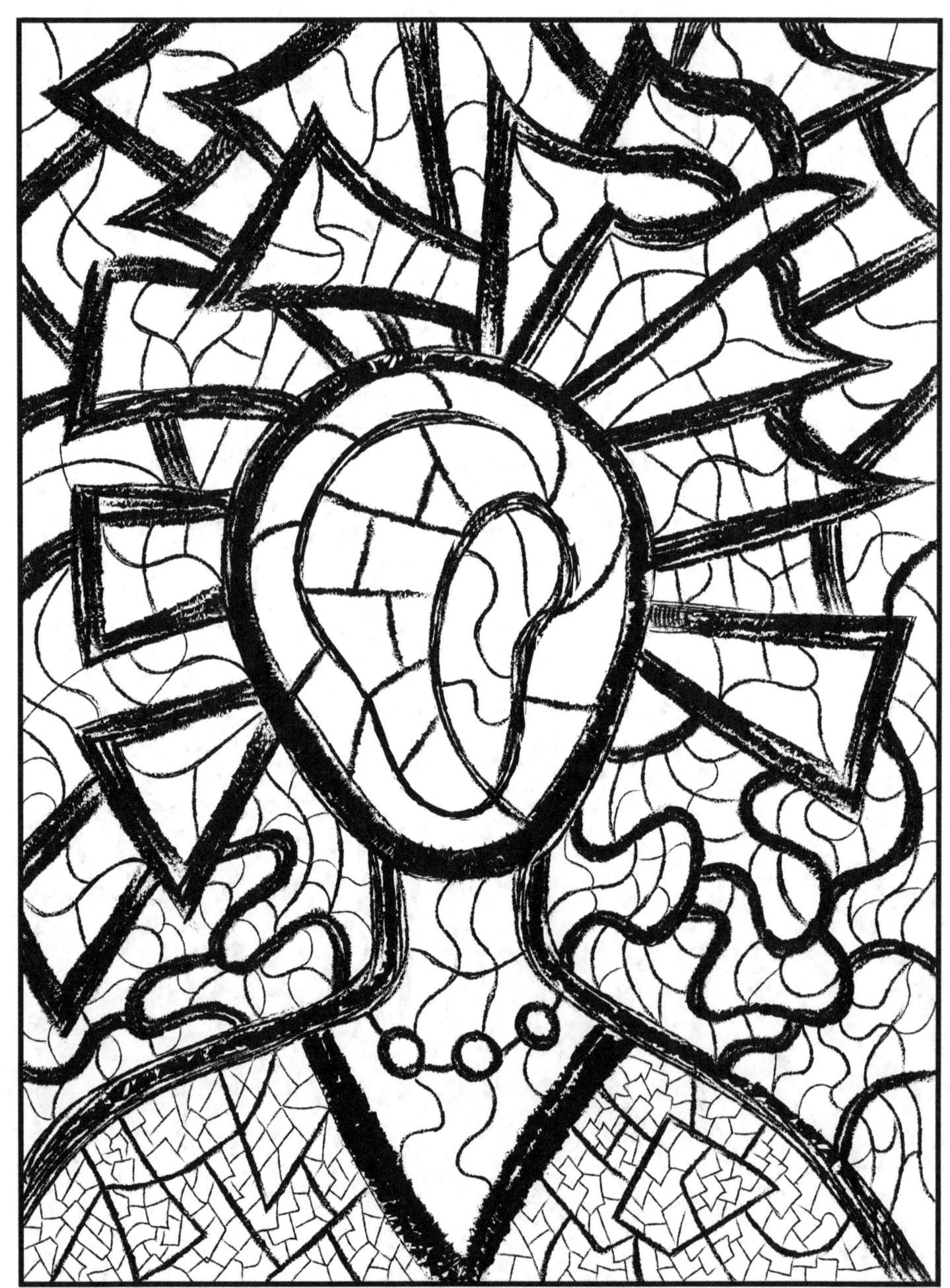

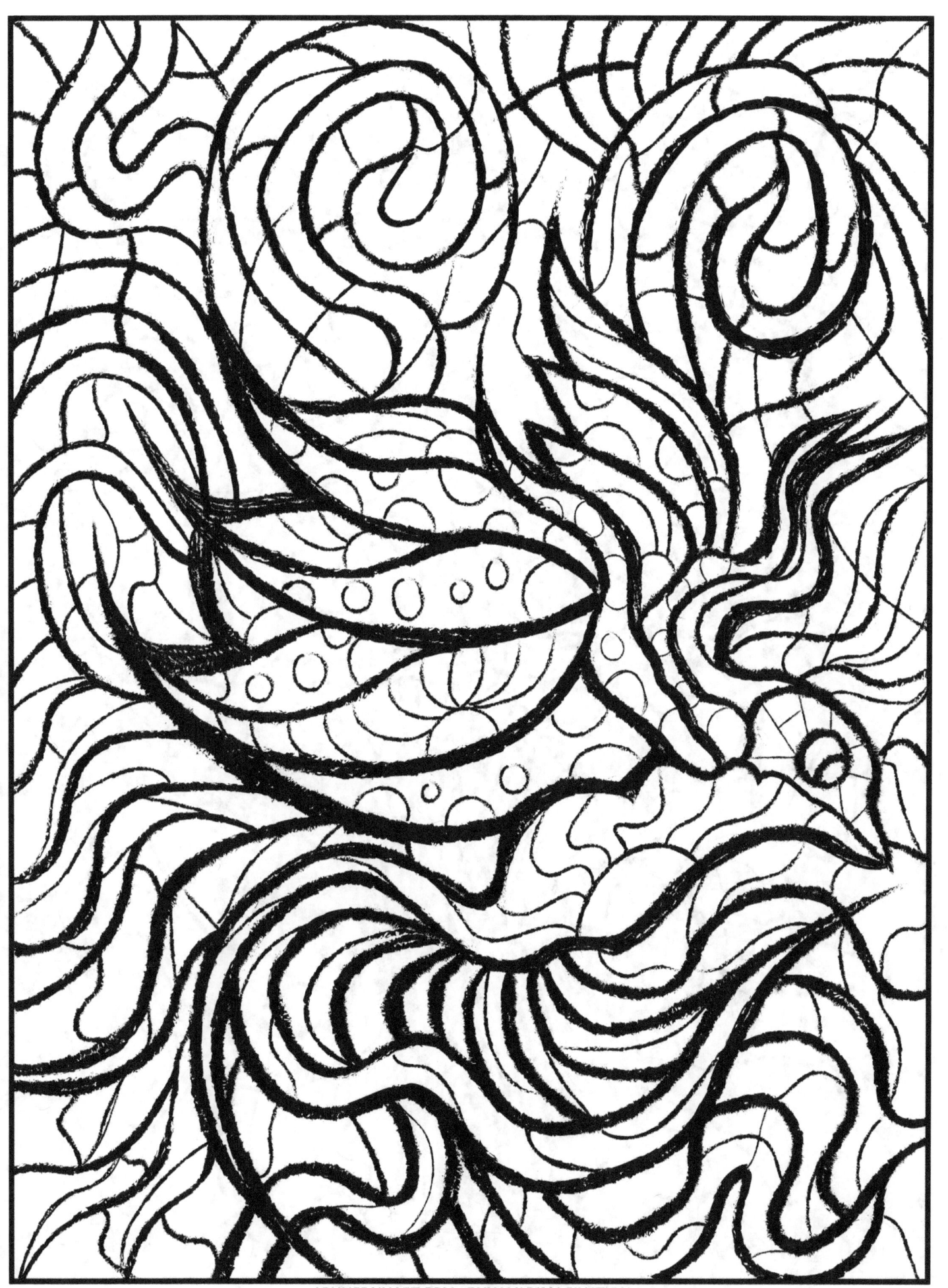

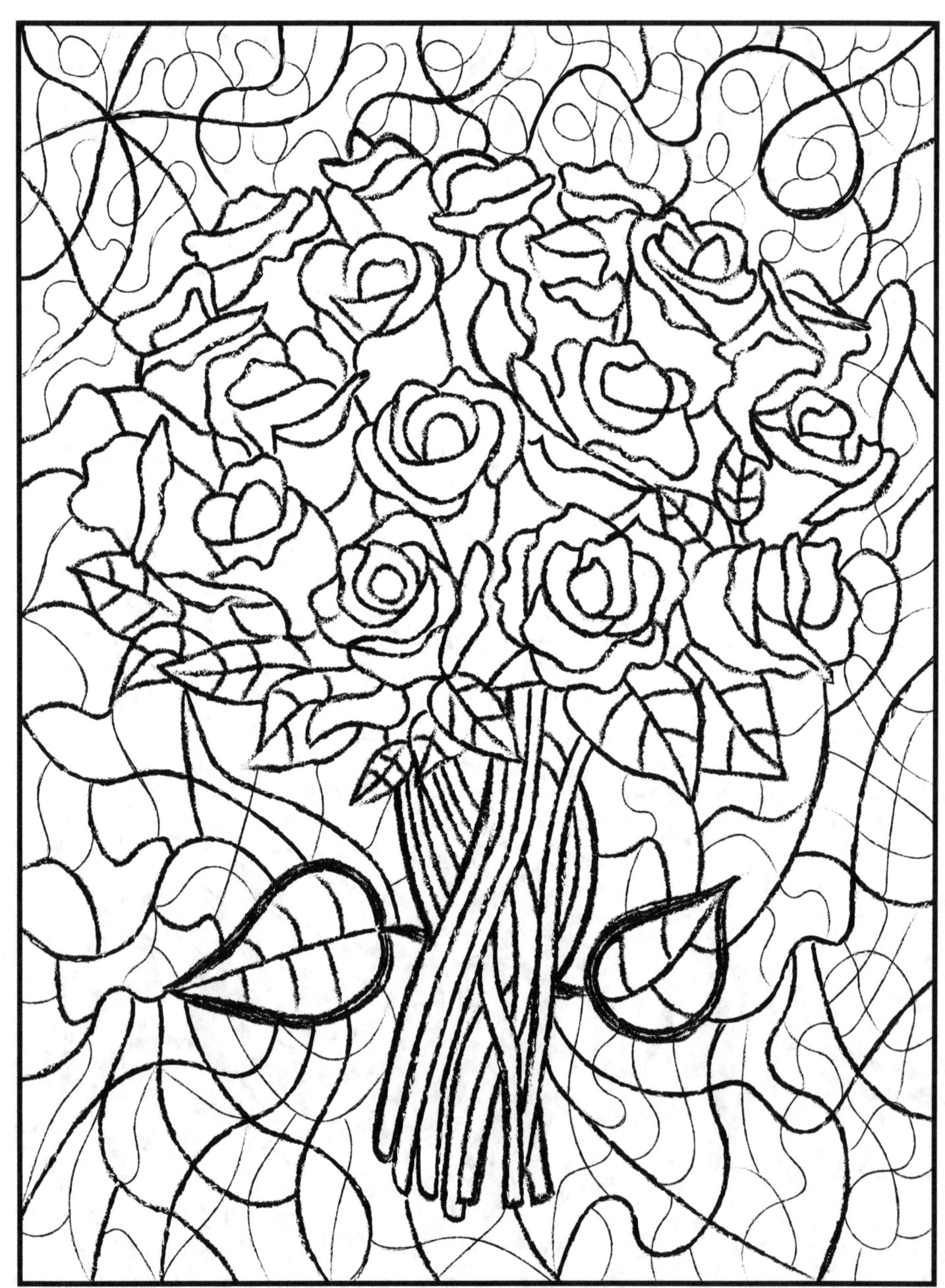

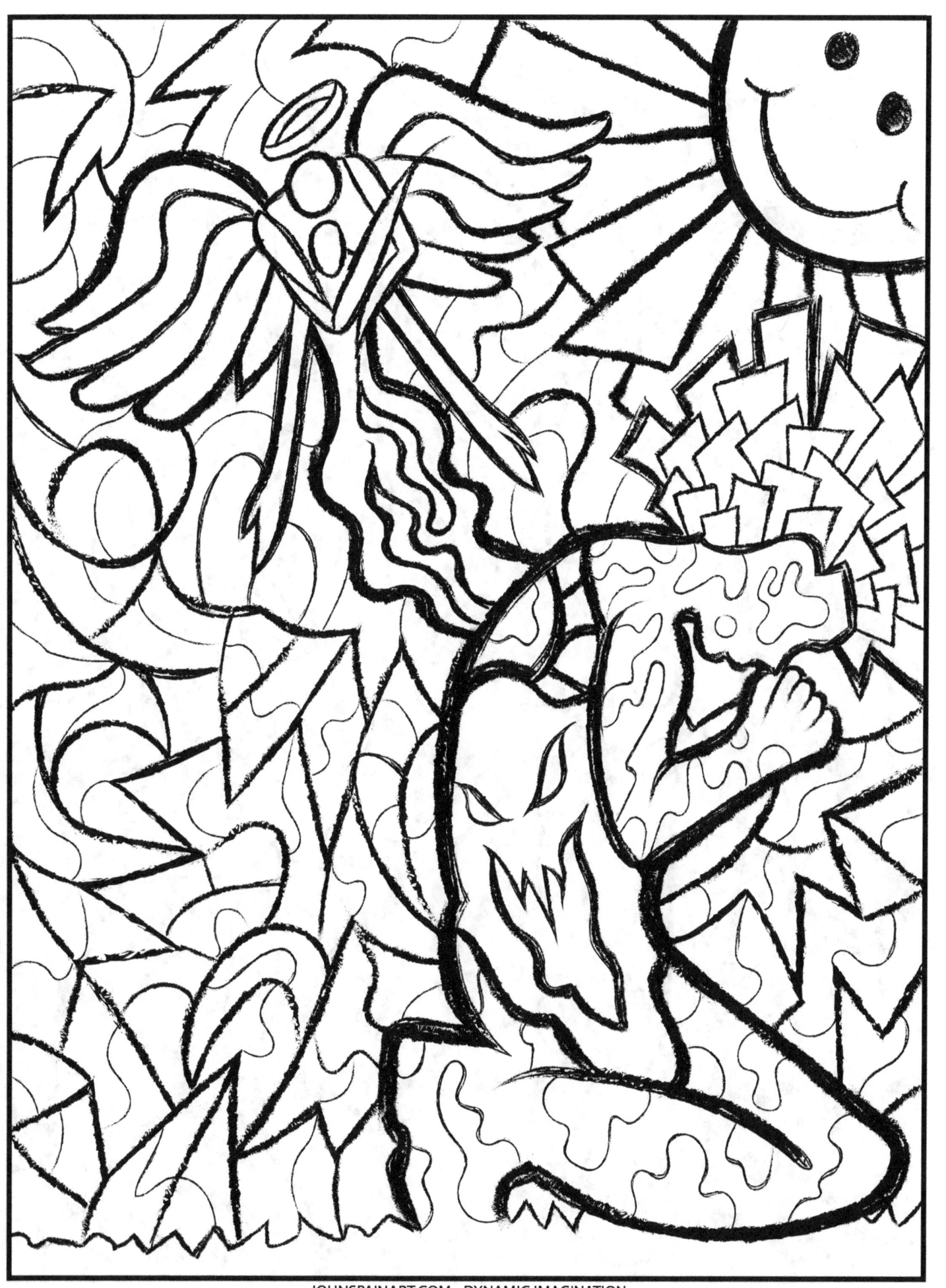

JOHNSPAINART.COM - DYNAMIC IMAGINATION

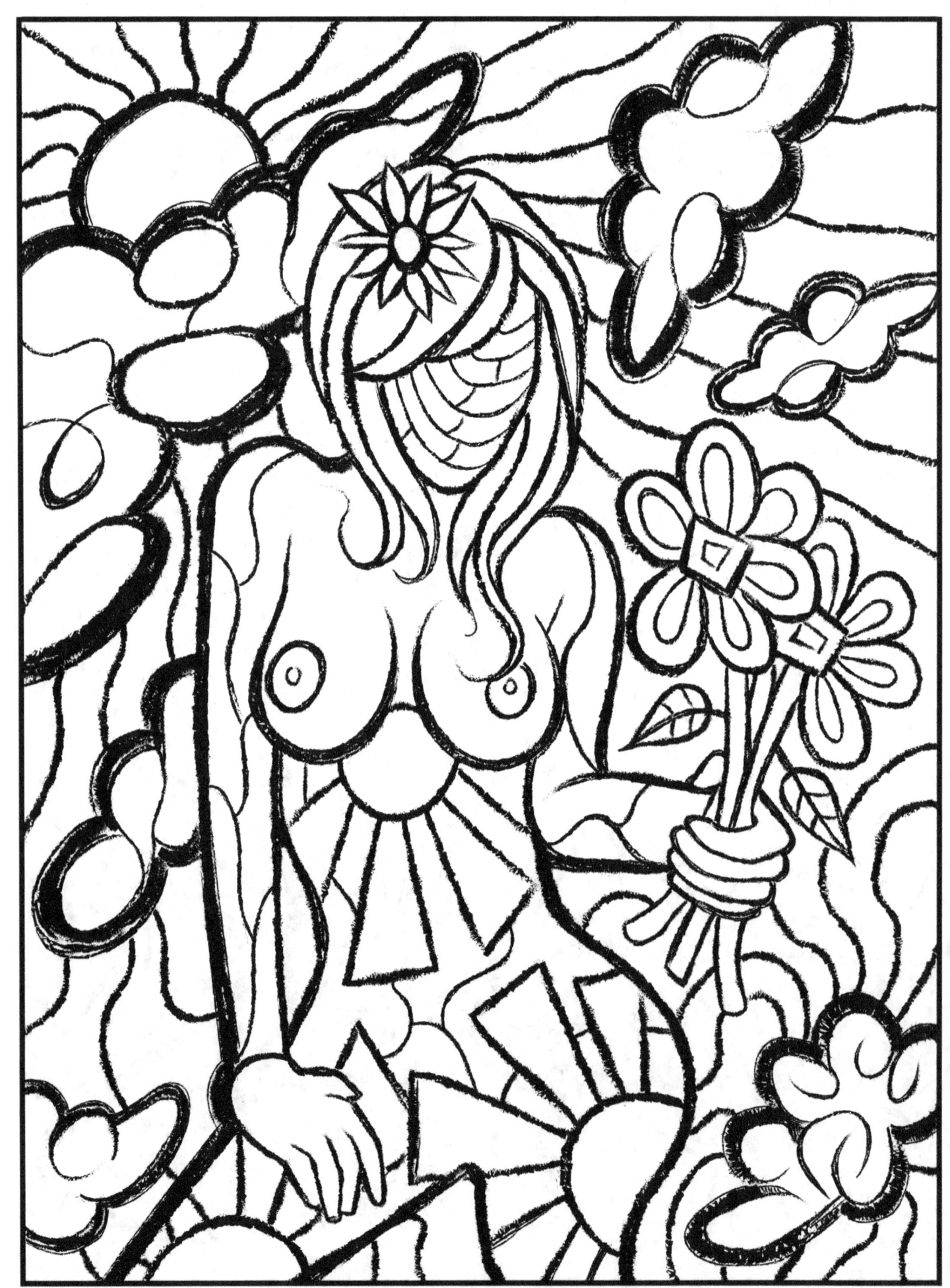

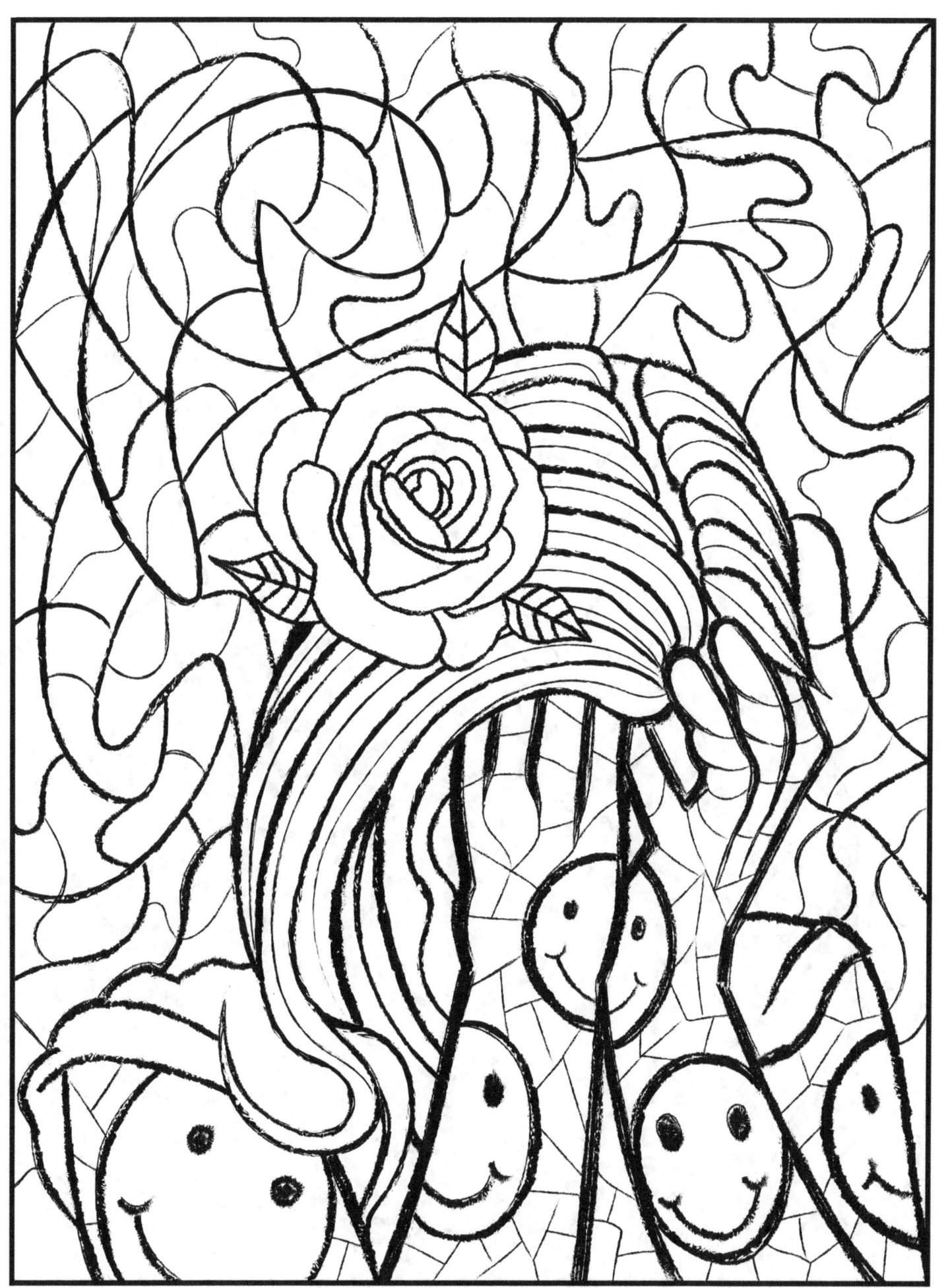

JOHNSPAINART.COM - DYNAMIC IMAGINATION

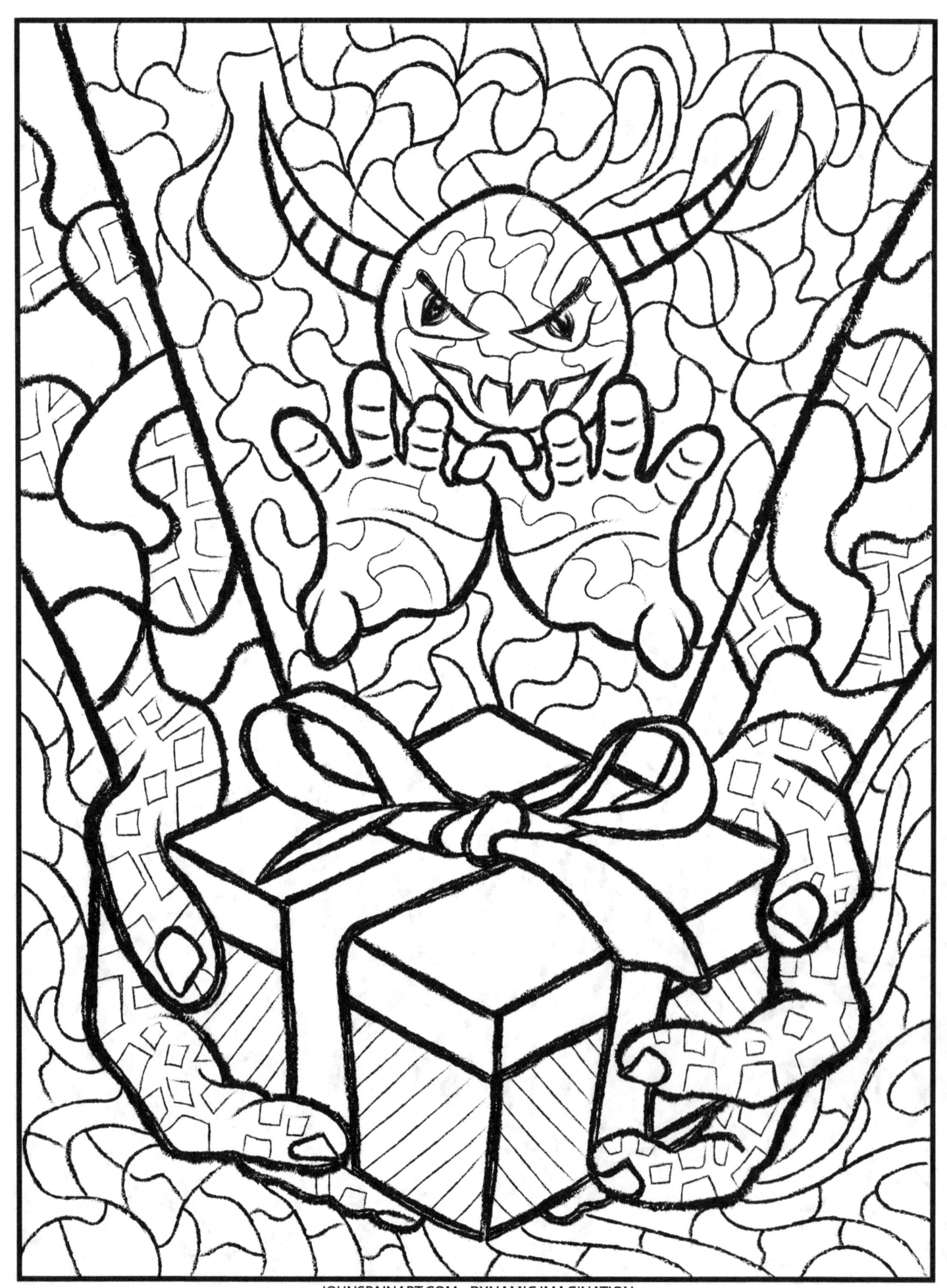
JOHNSPAINART.COM - DYNAMIC IMAGINATION

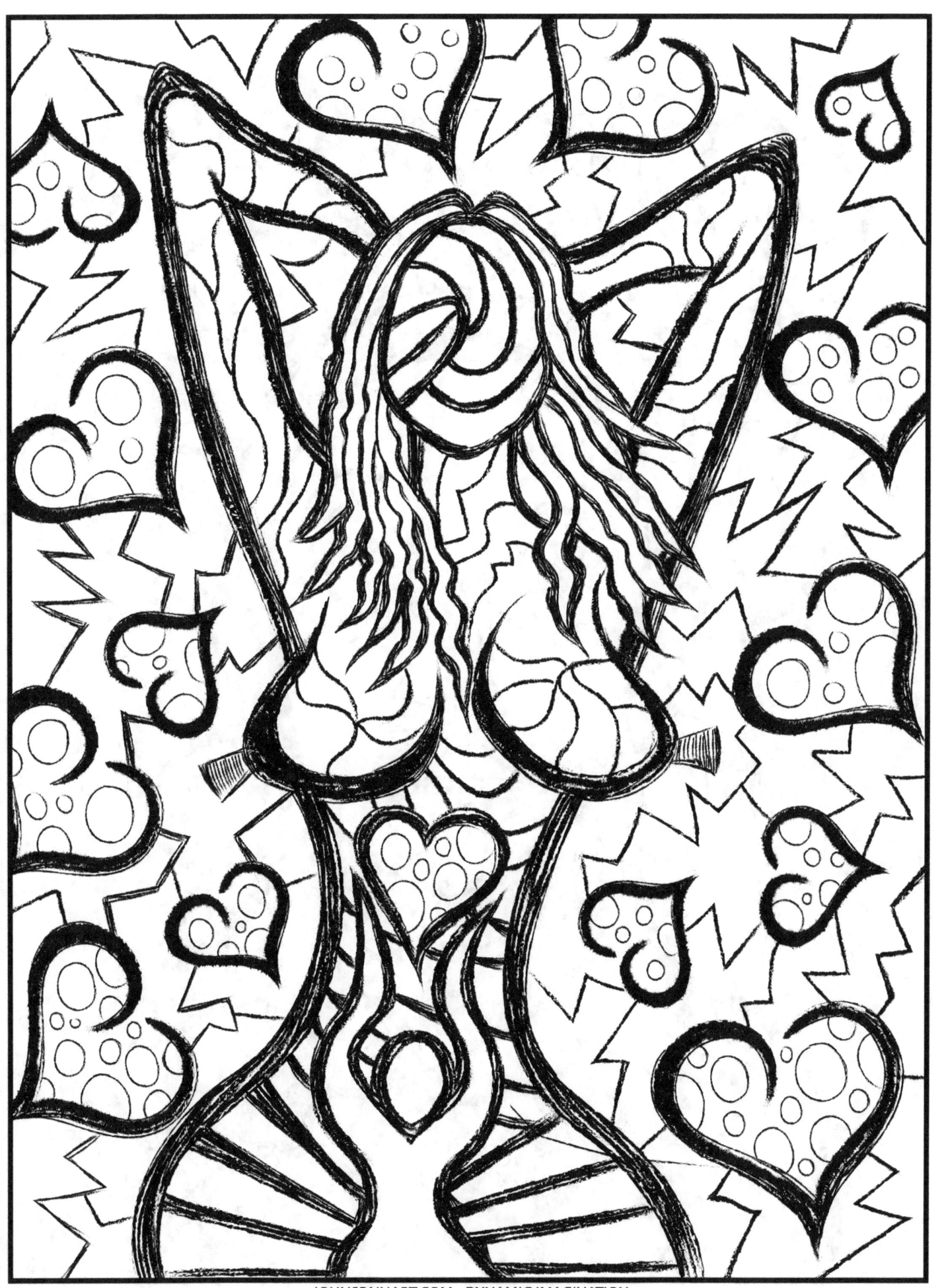

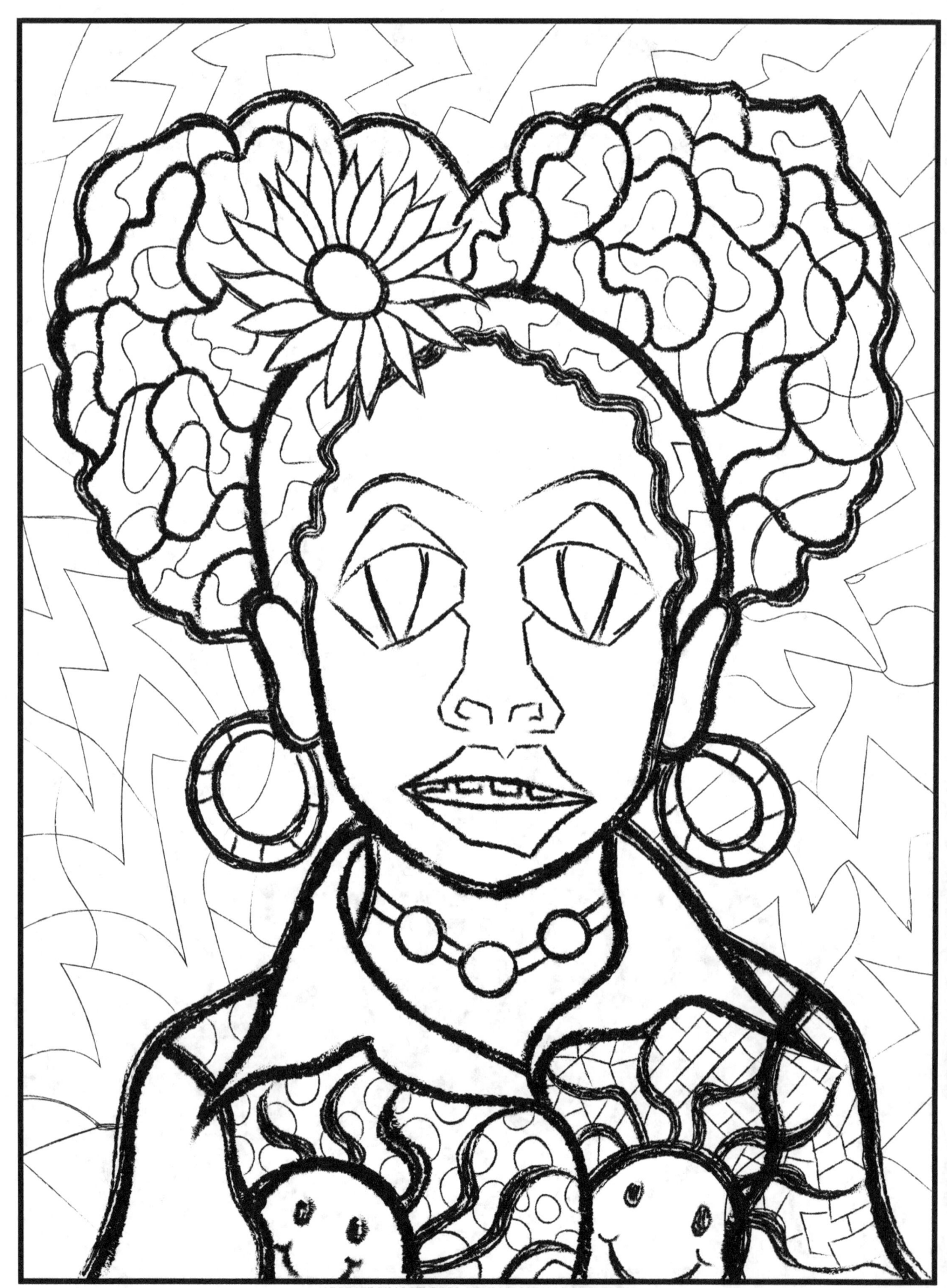

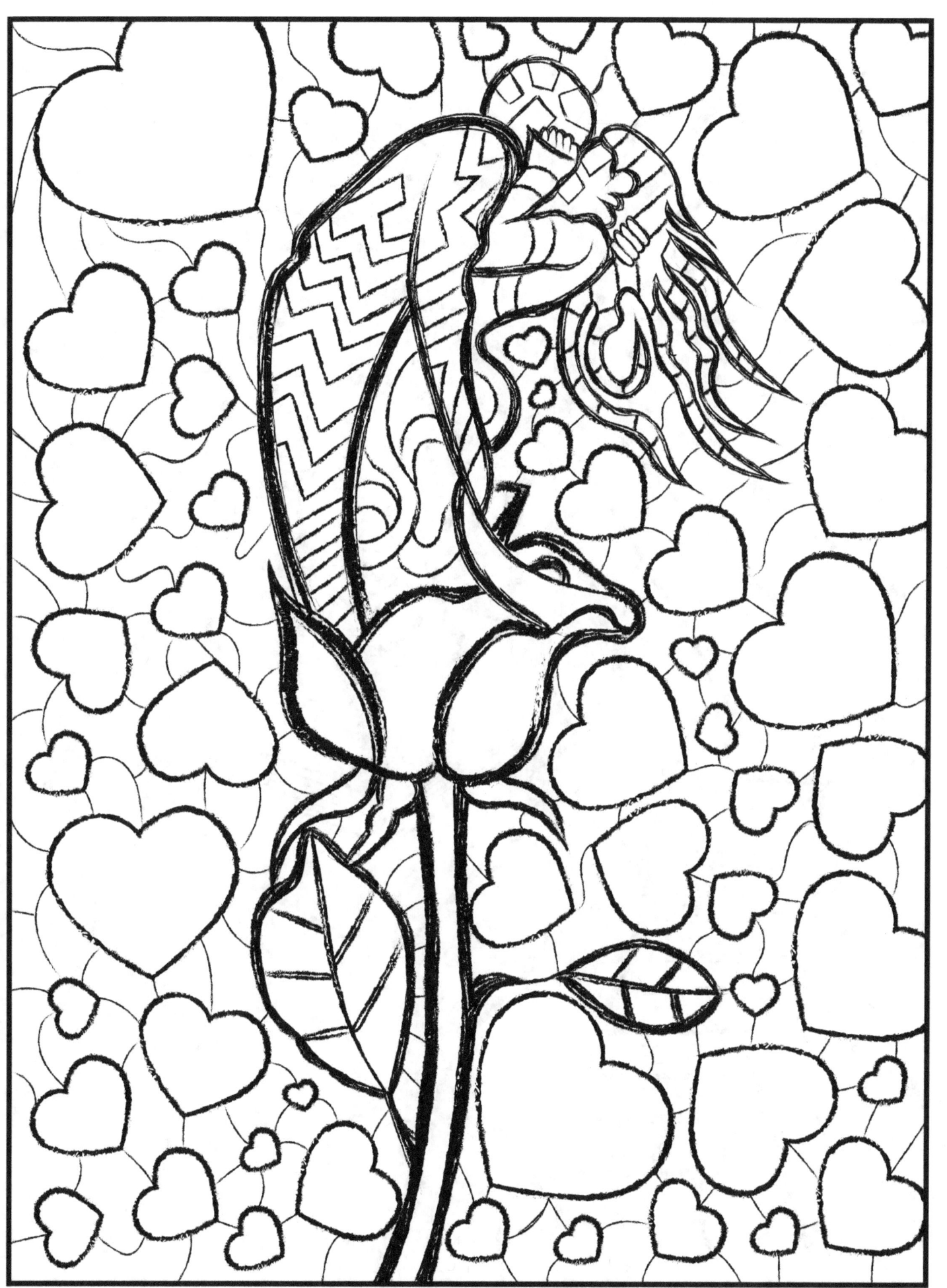

JOHNSPAINART.COM - DYNAMIC IMAGINATION

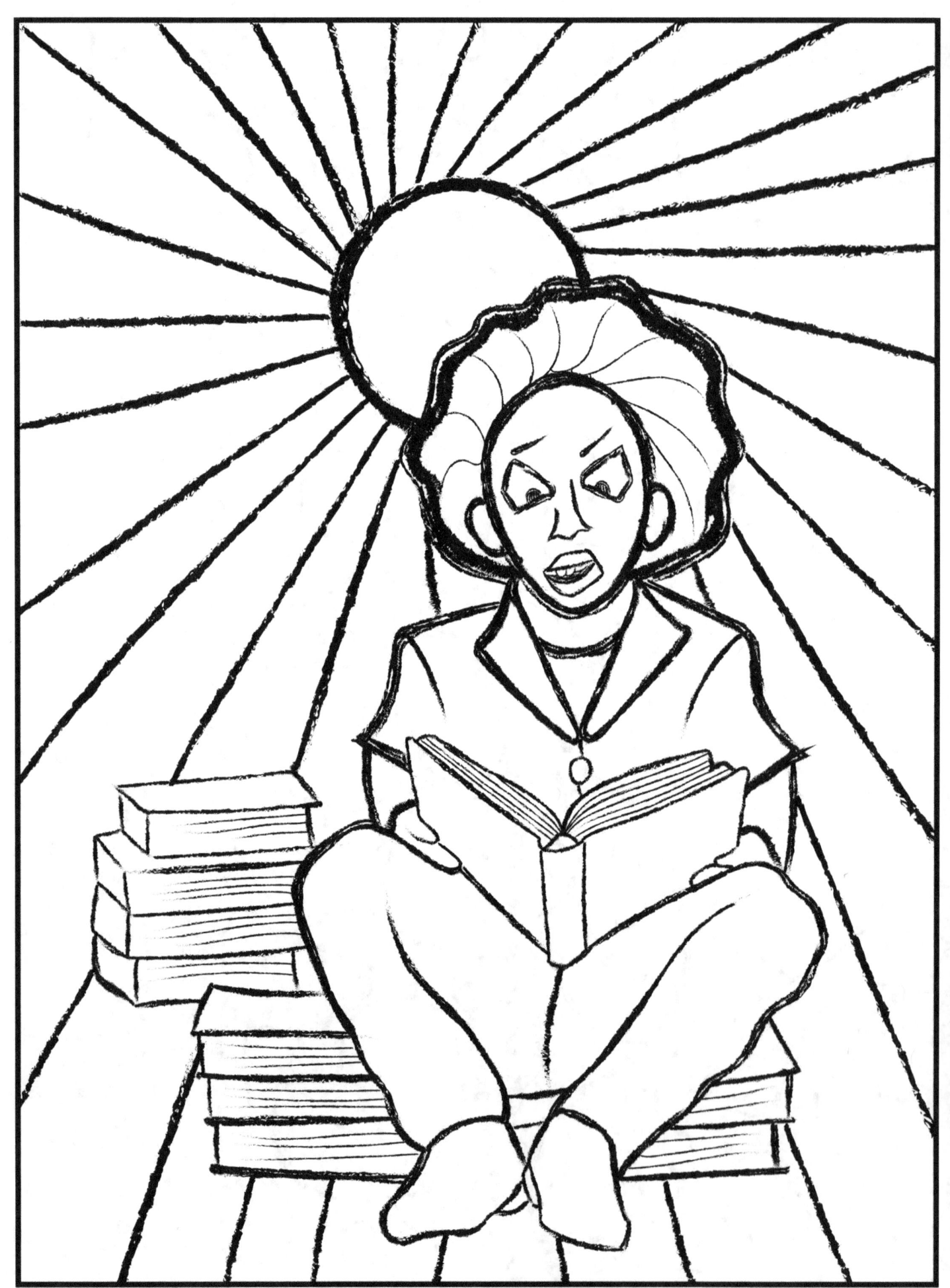

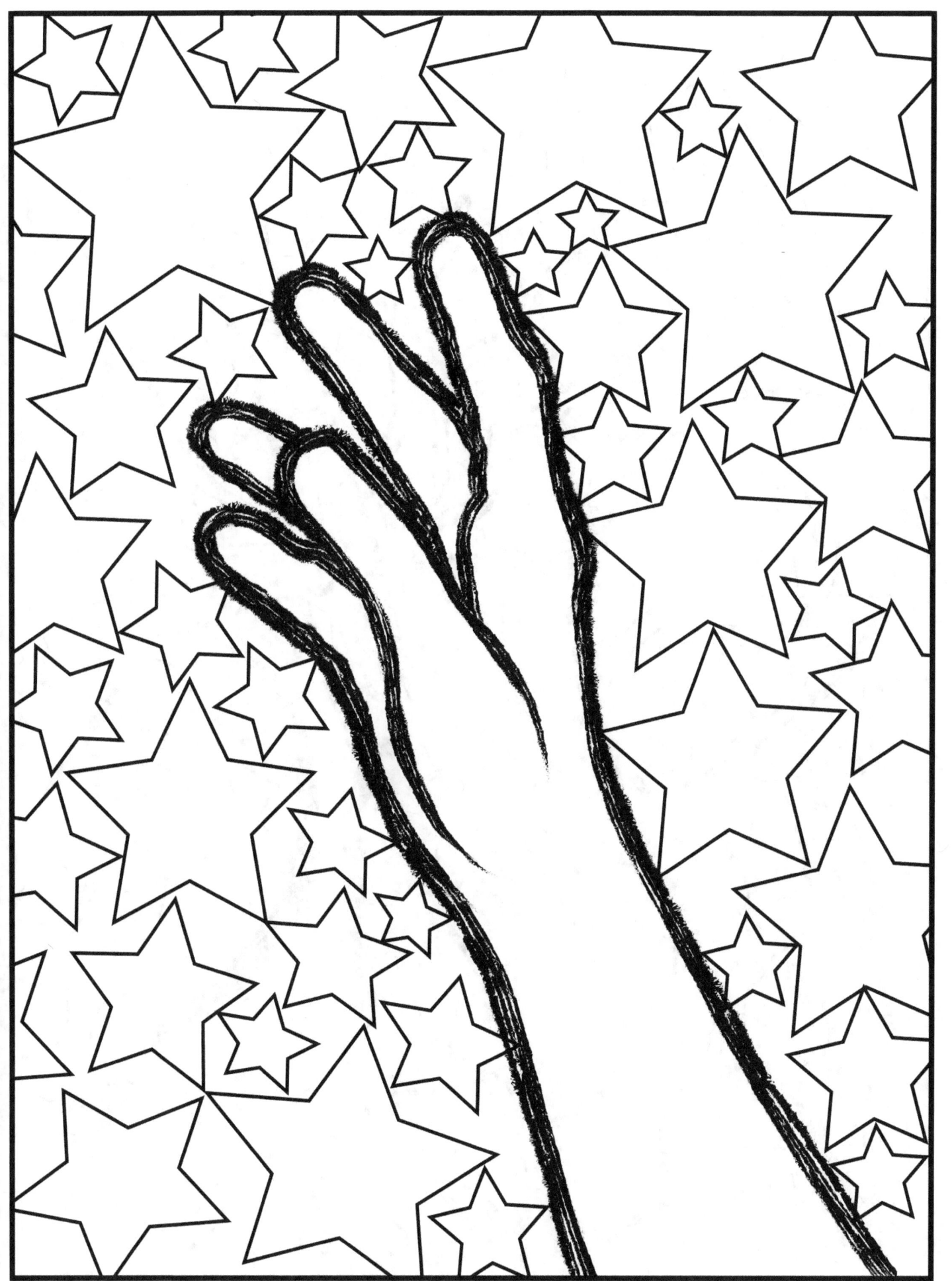

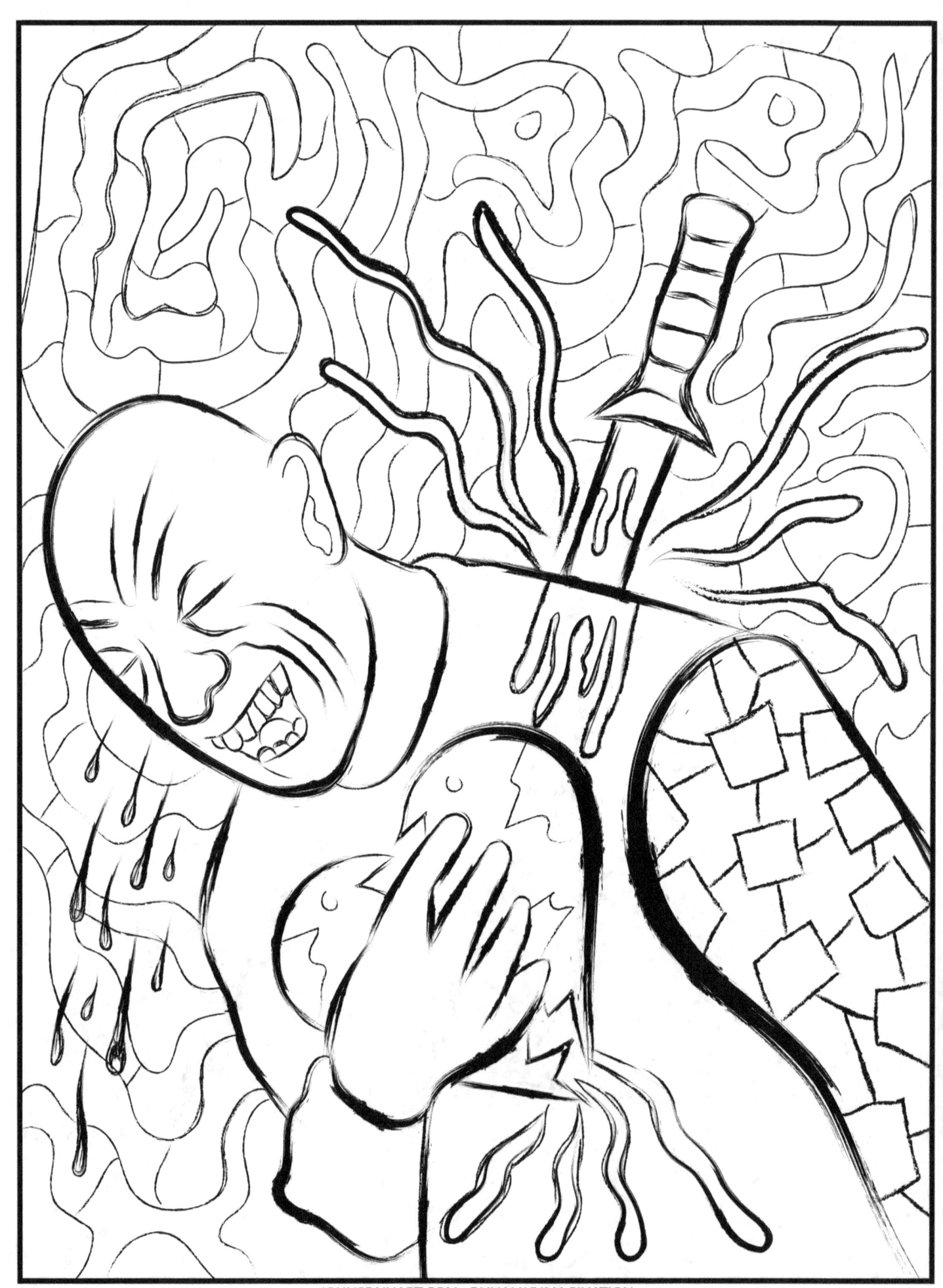

JOHNSPAINART.COM - DYNAMIC IMAGINATION

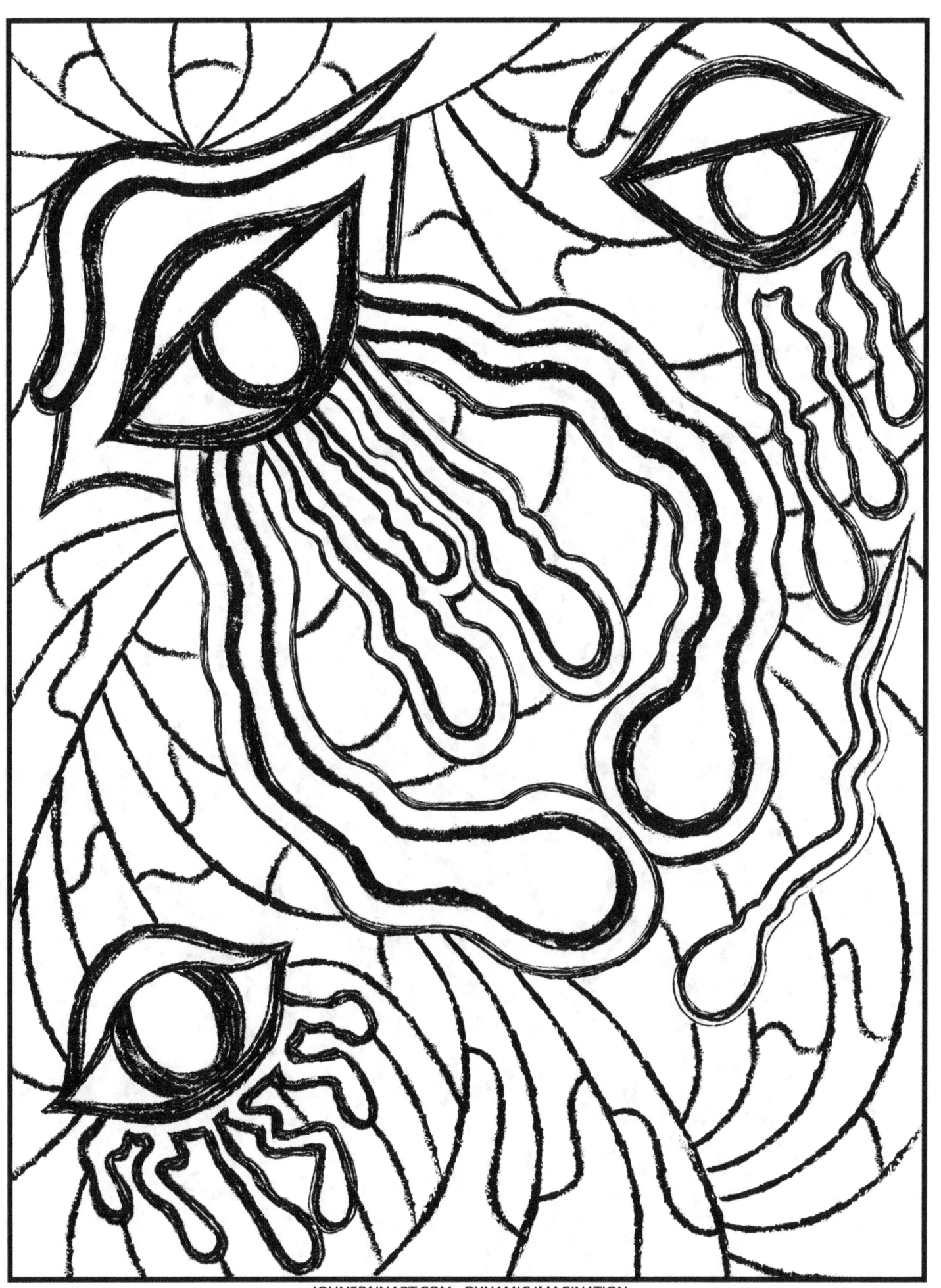

JOHNSPAINART.COM - DYNAMIC IMAGINATION

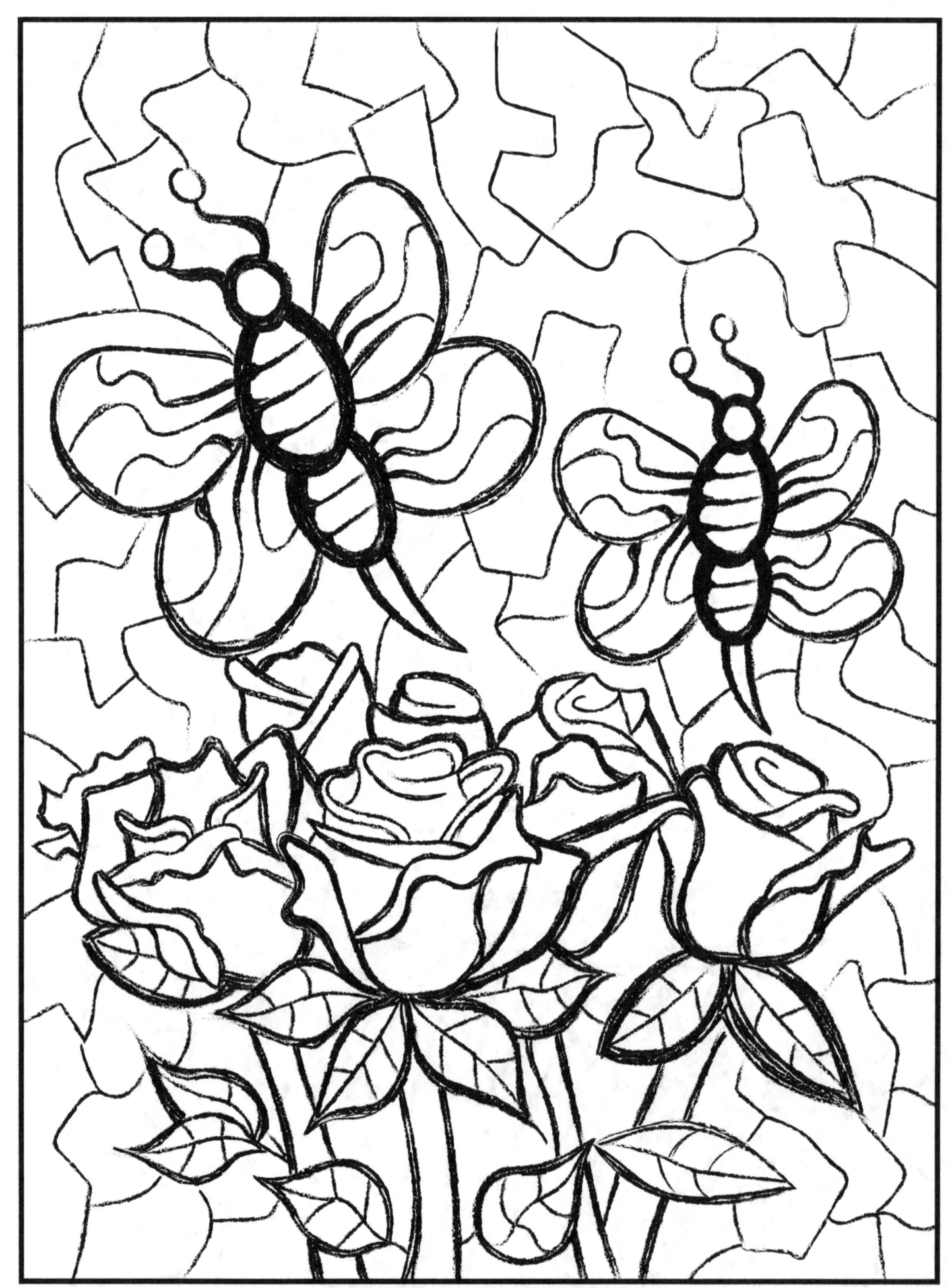

JOHNSPAINART.COM - DYNAMIC IMAGINATION

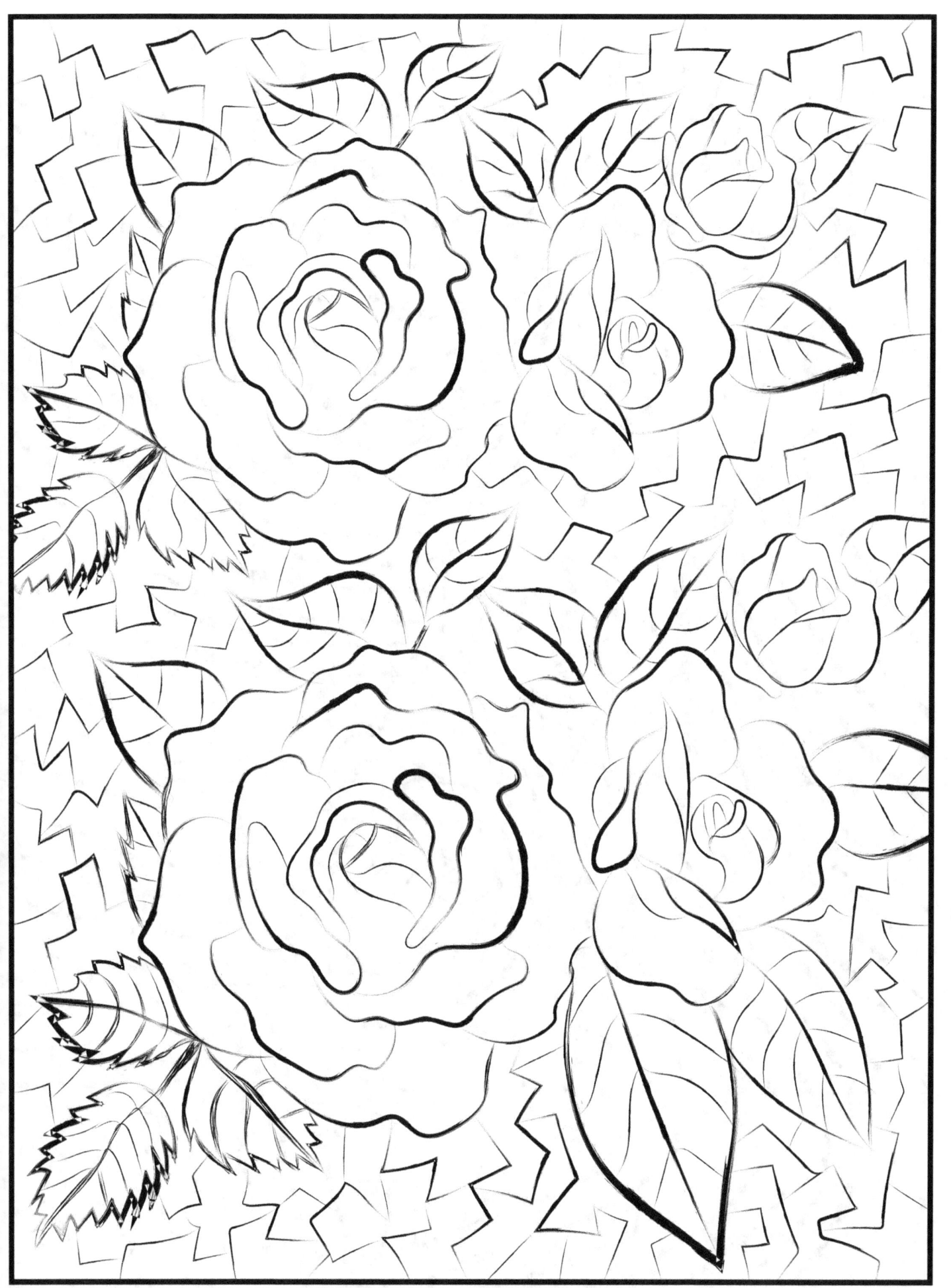
JOHNSPAINART.COM - DYNAMIC IMAGINATION

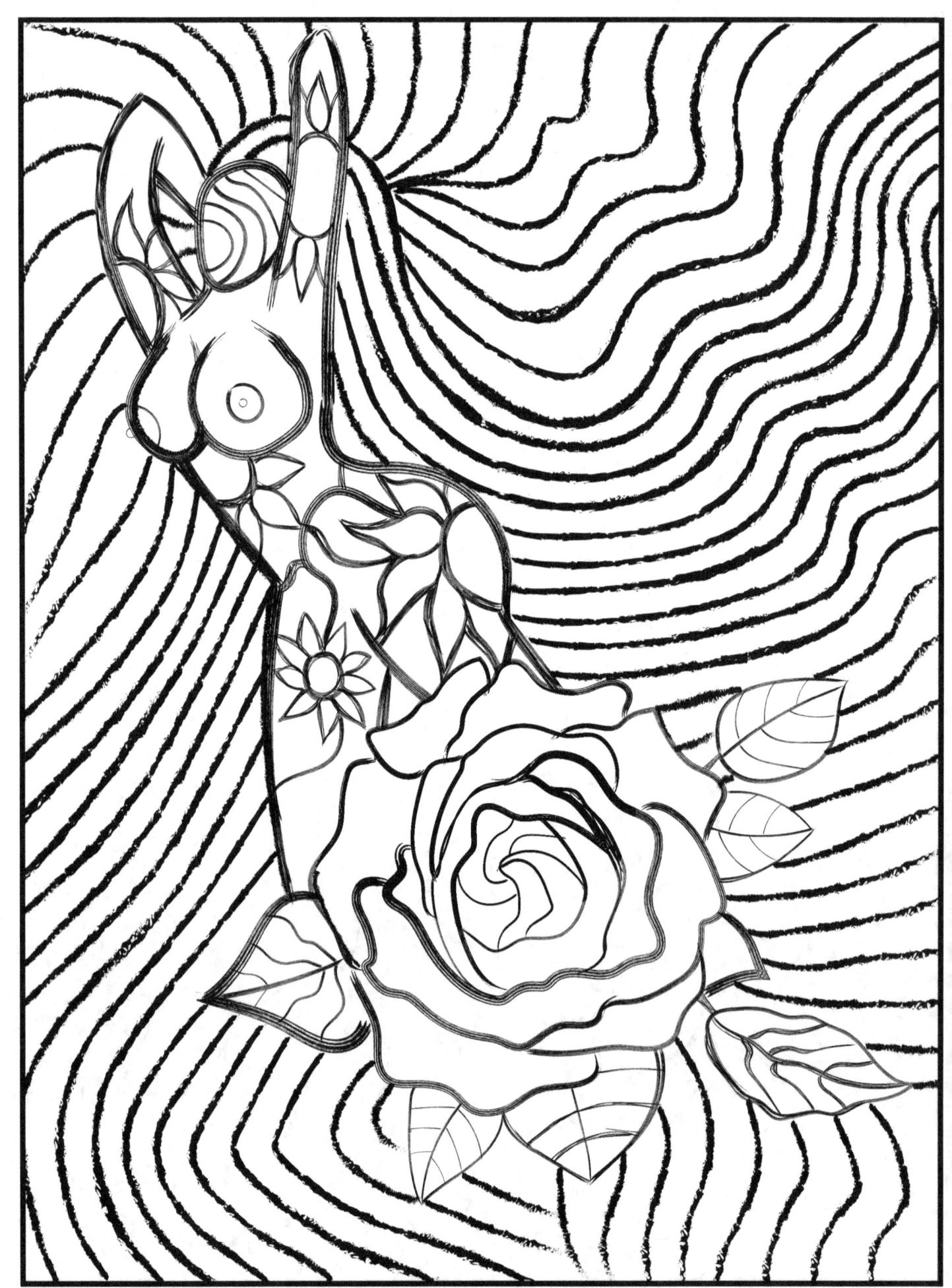

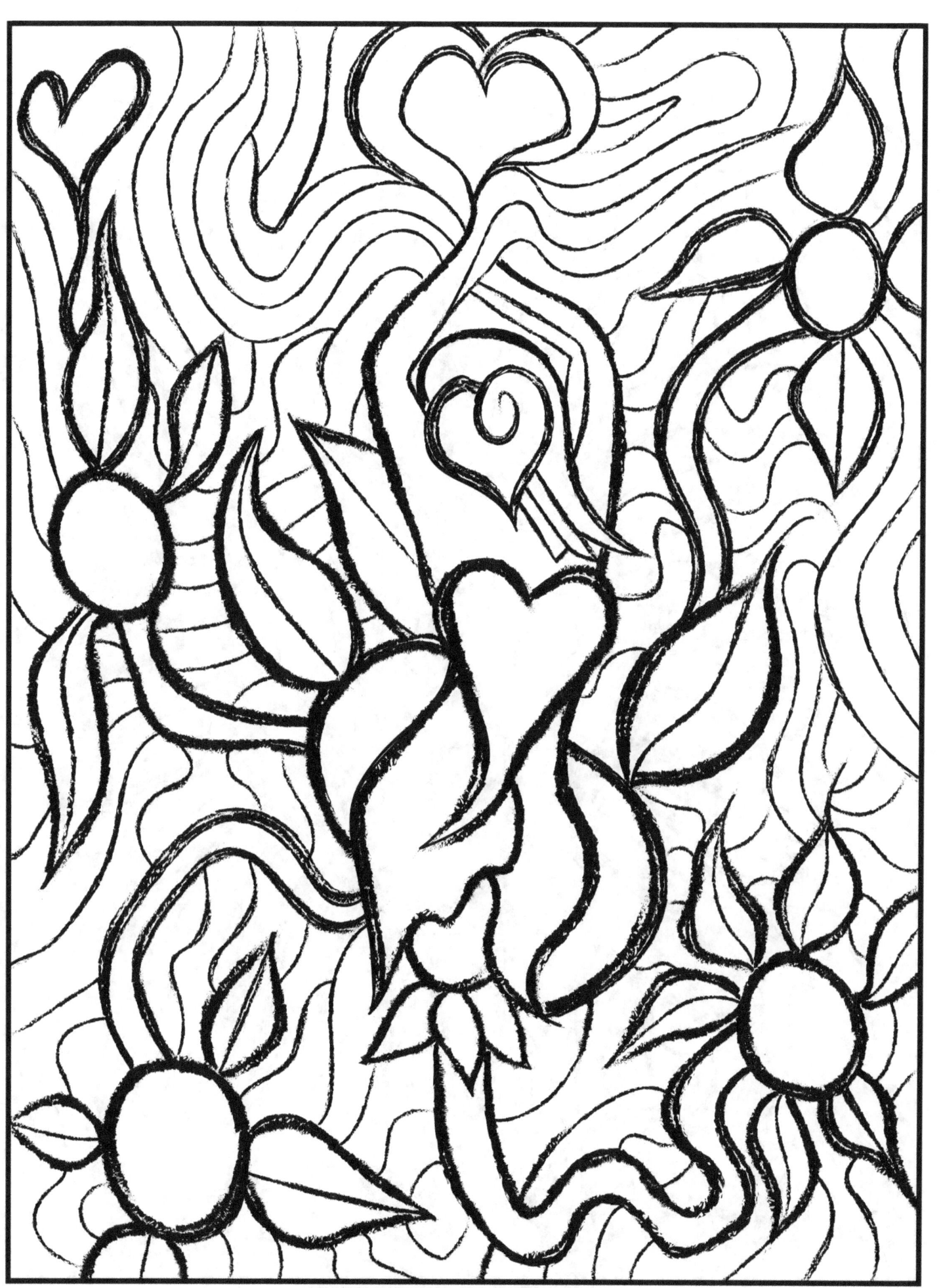

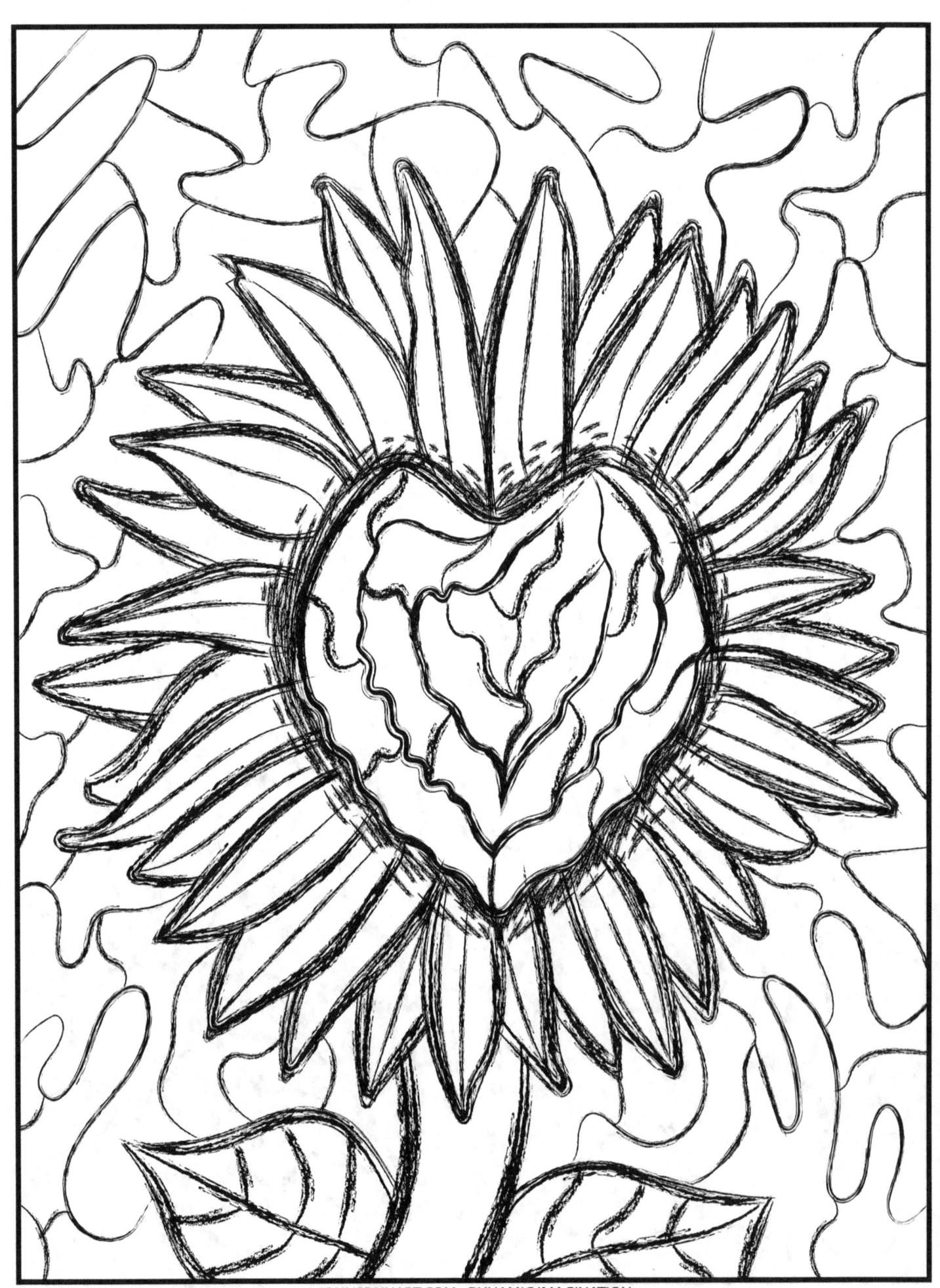

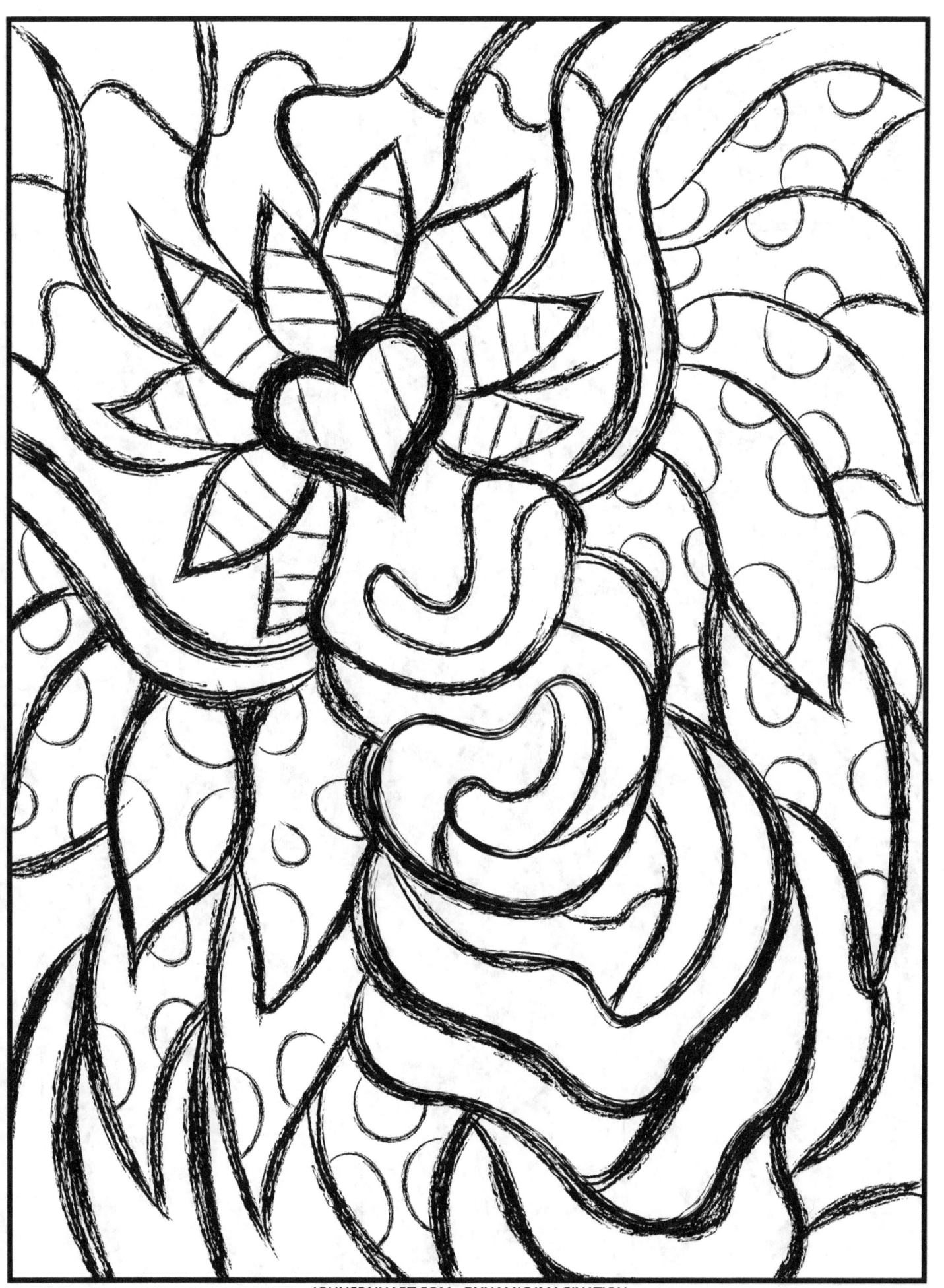

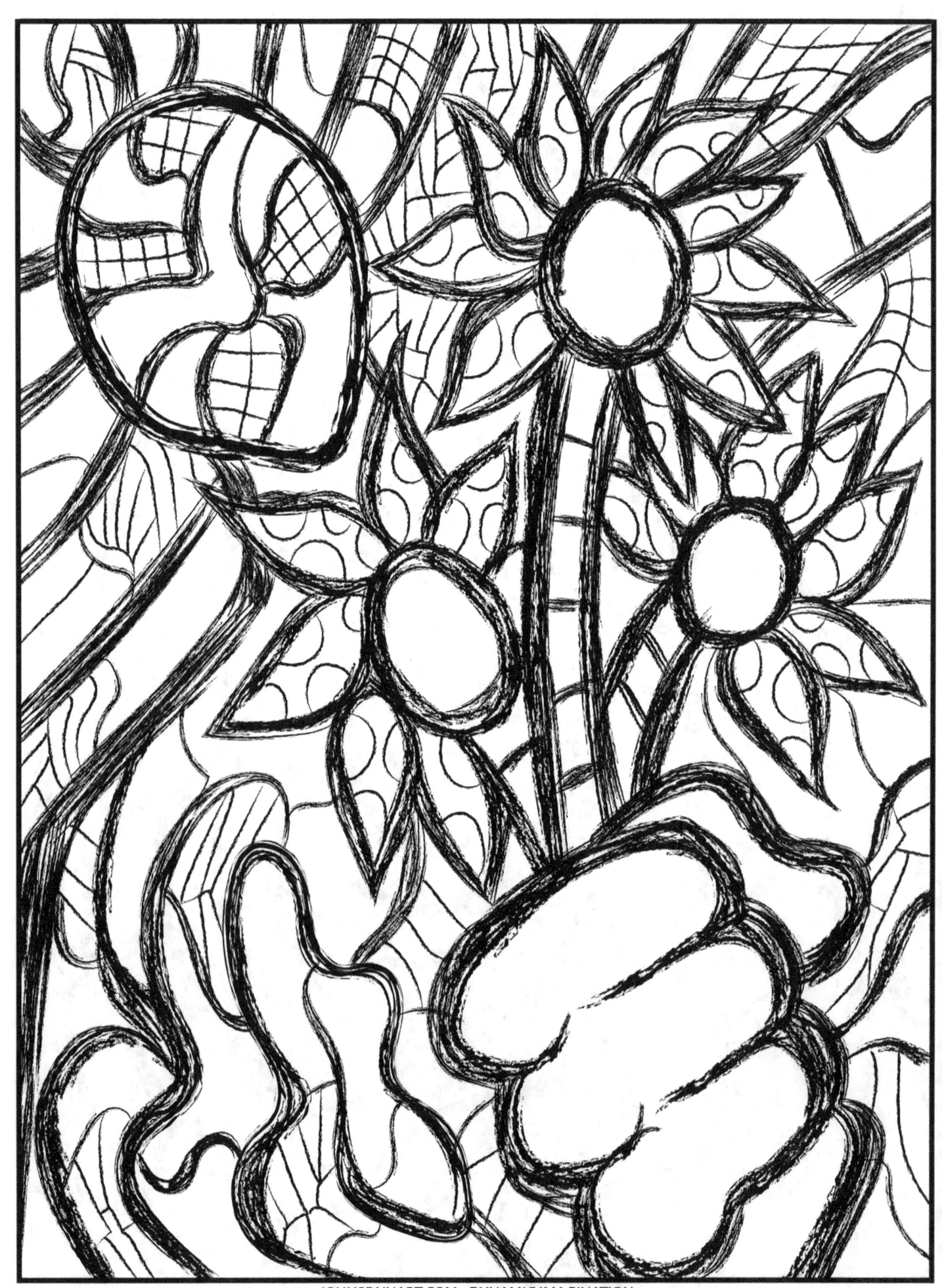

JOHNSPAINART.COM - DYNAMIC IMAGINATION

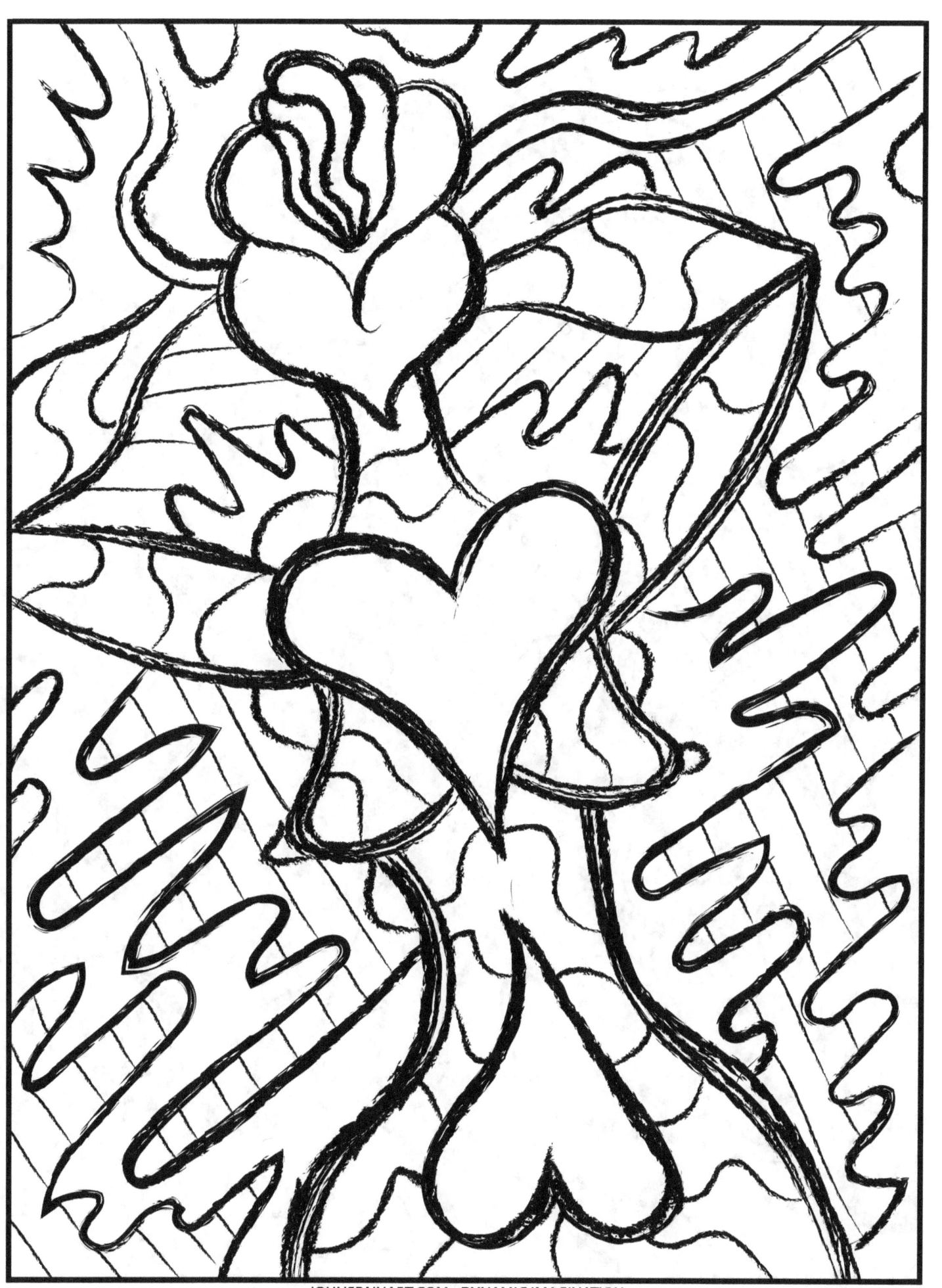

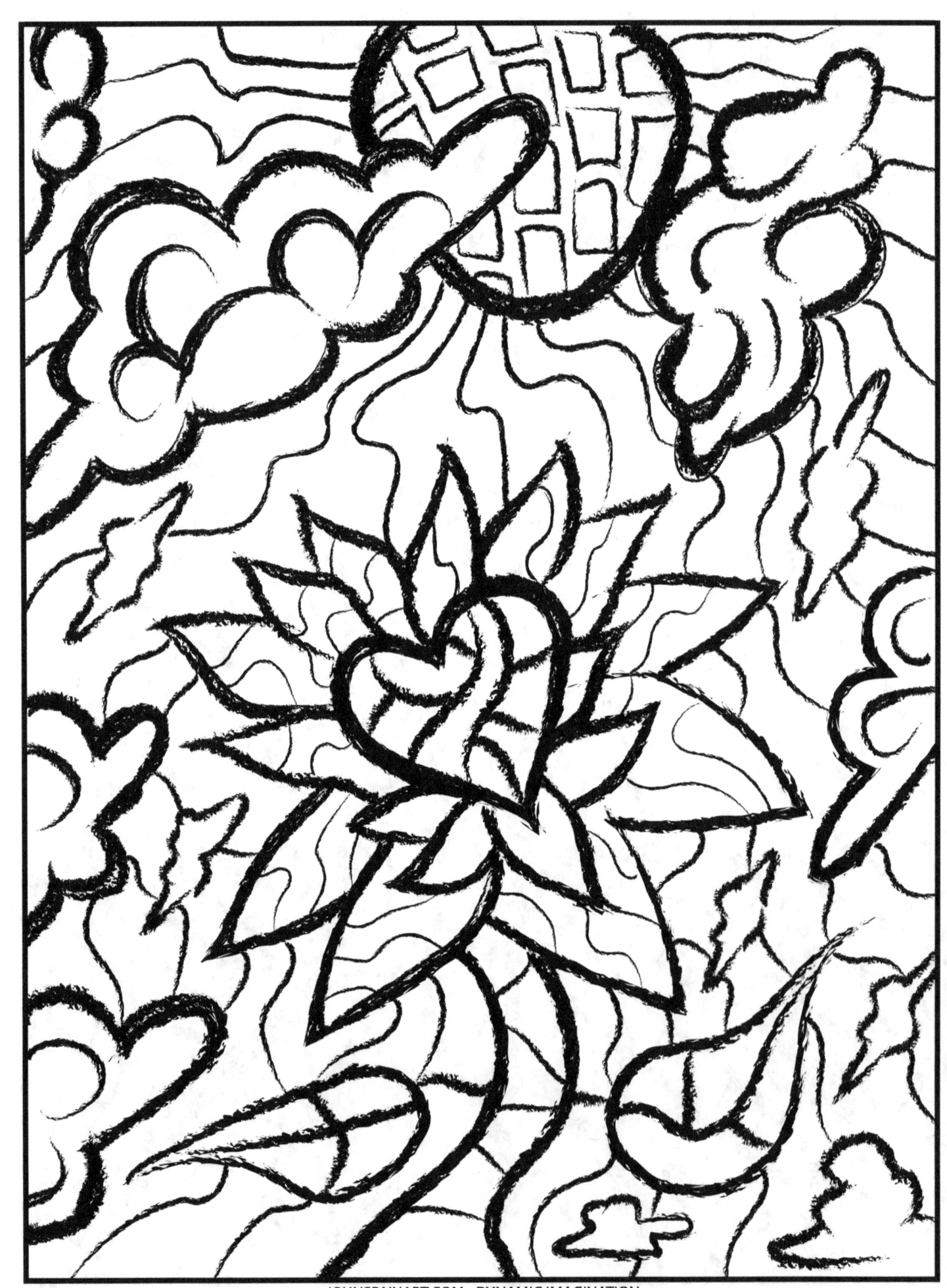
JOHNSPAINART.COM - DYNAMIC IMAGINATION

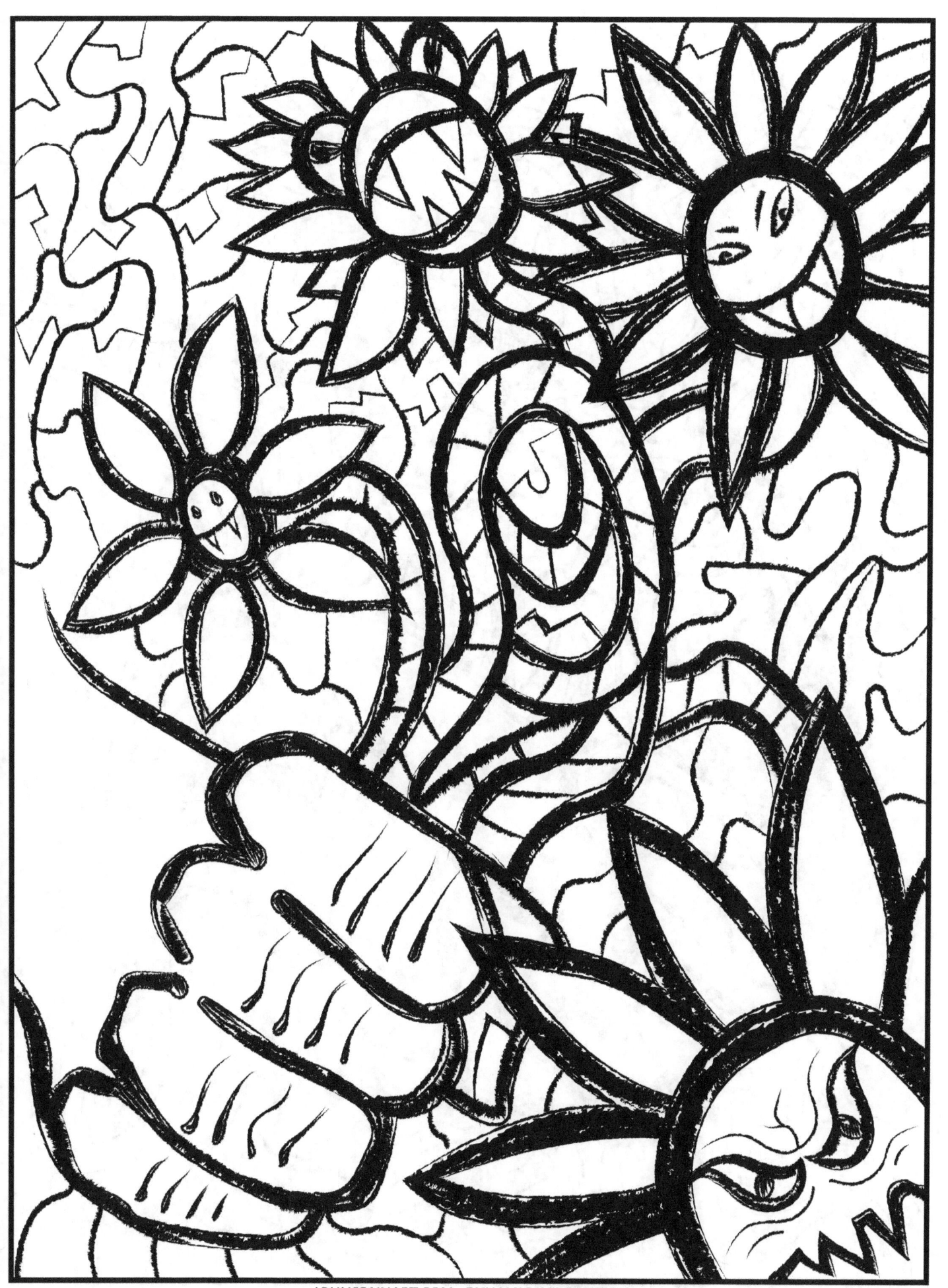

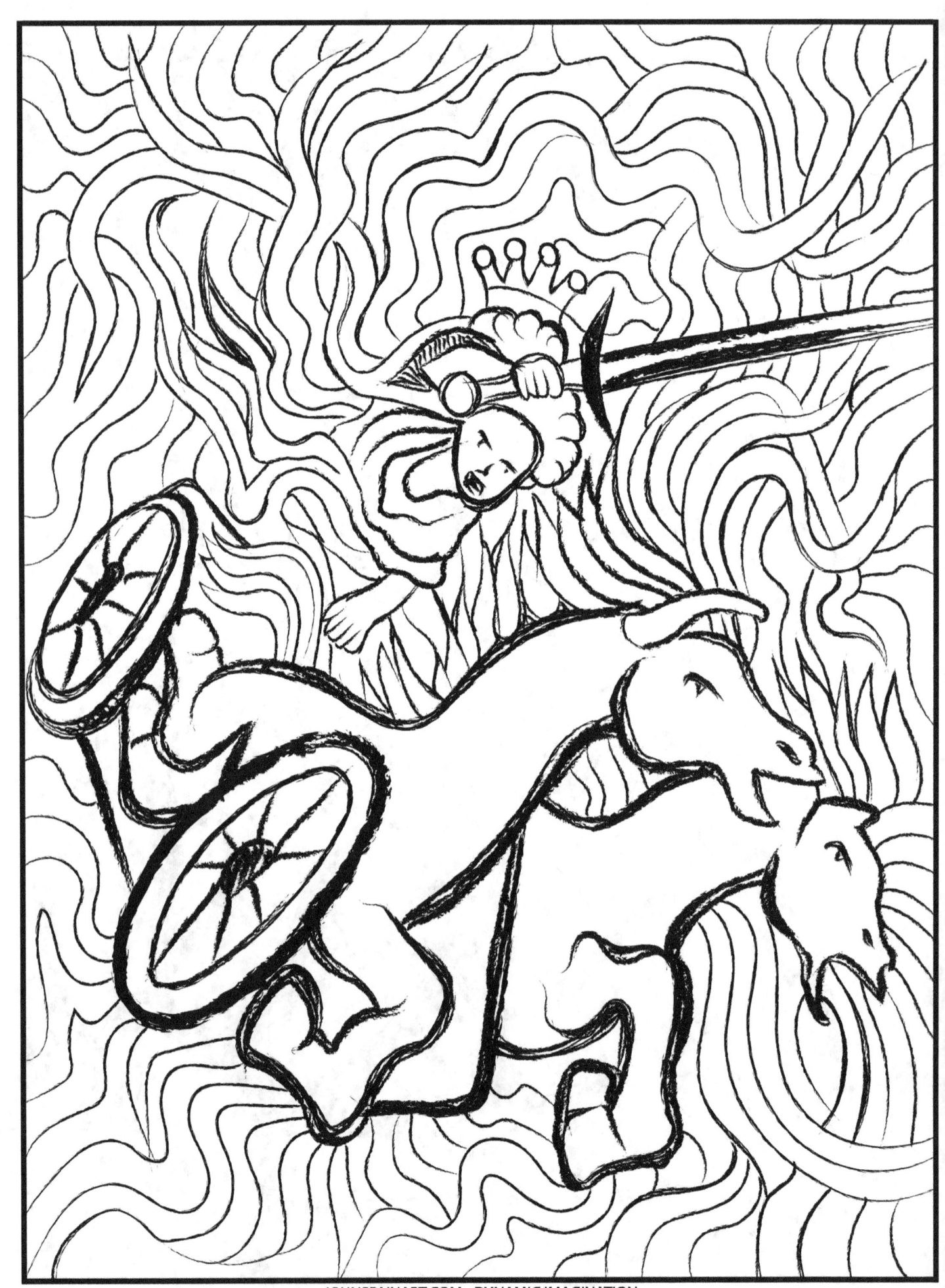

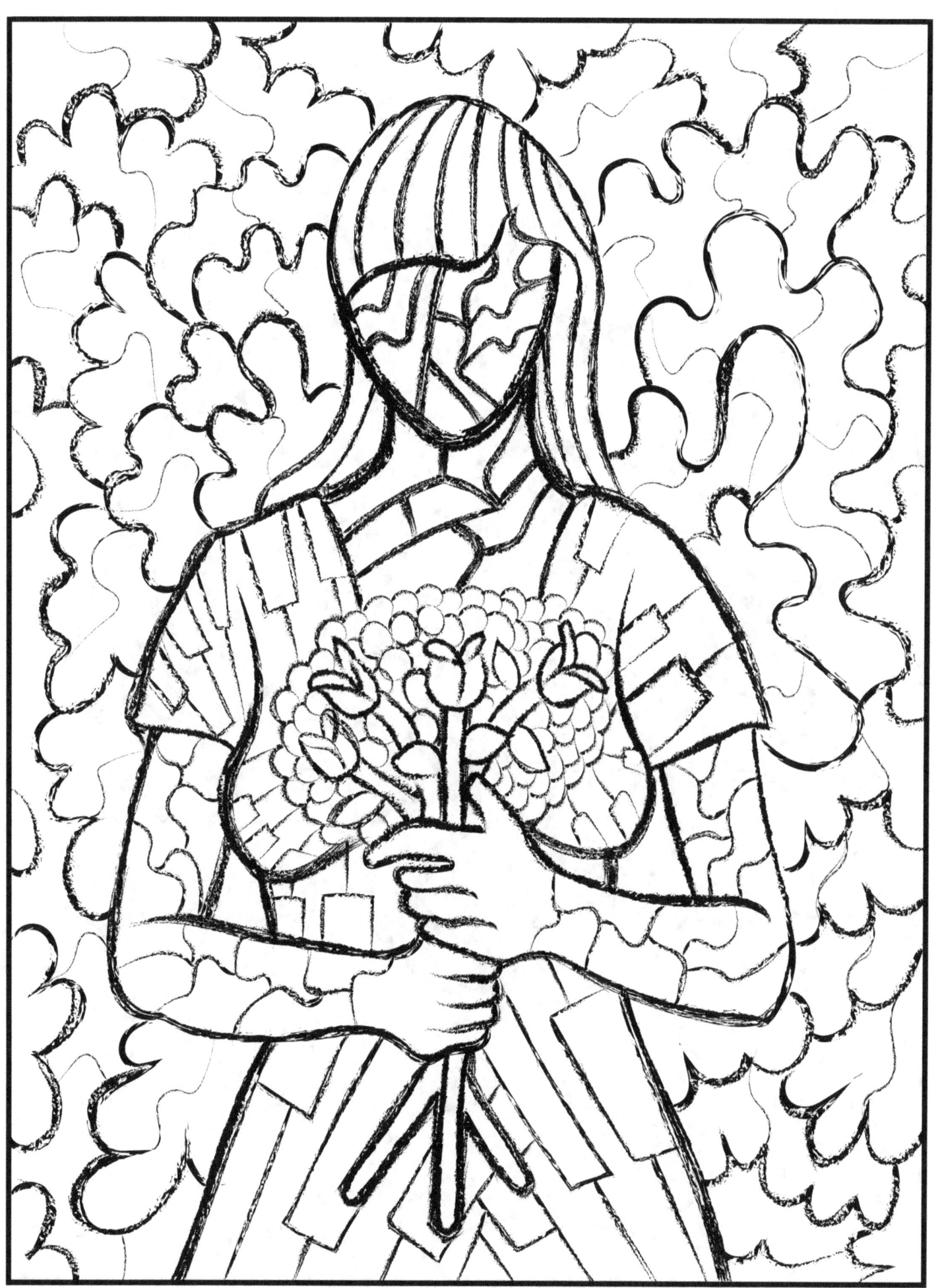

JOHNSPAINART.COM - DYNAMIC IMAGINATION

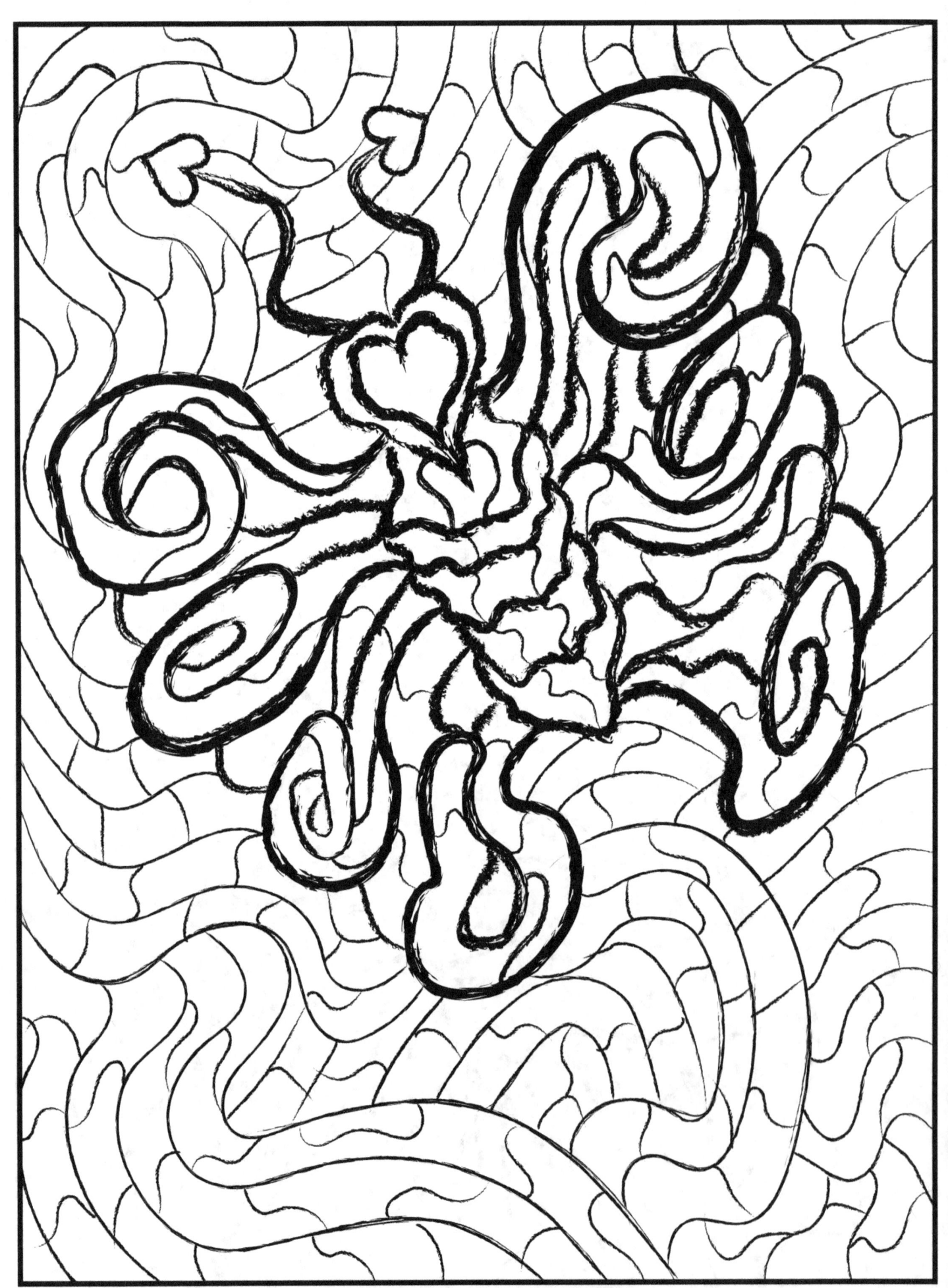

JOHNSPAINART.COM - DYNAMIC IMAGINATION

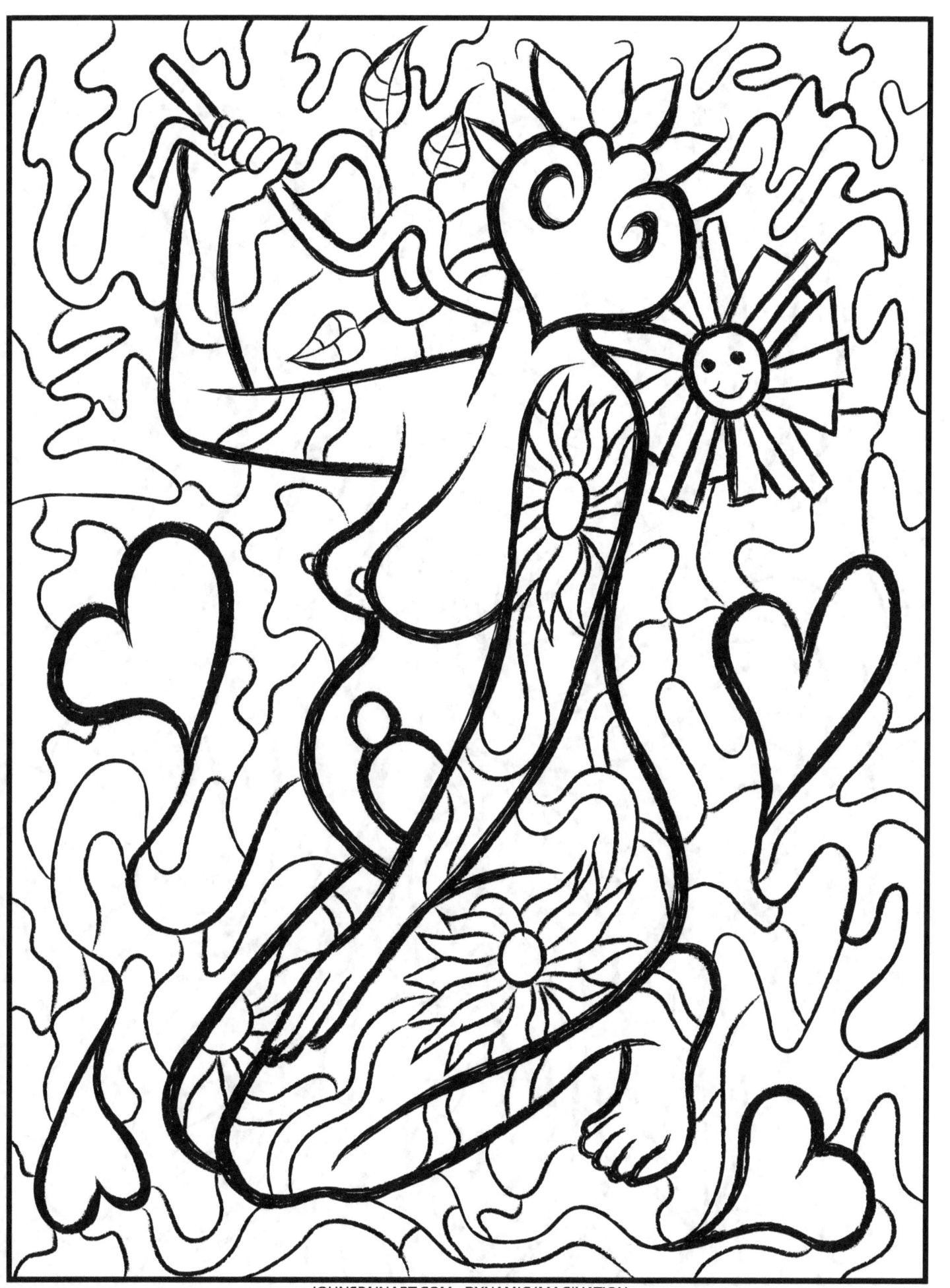

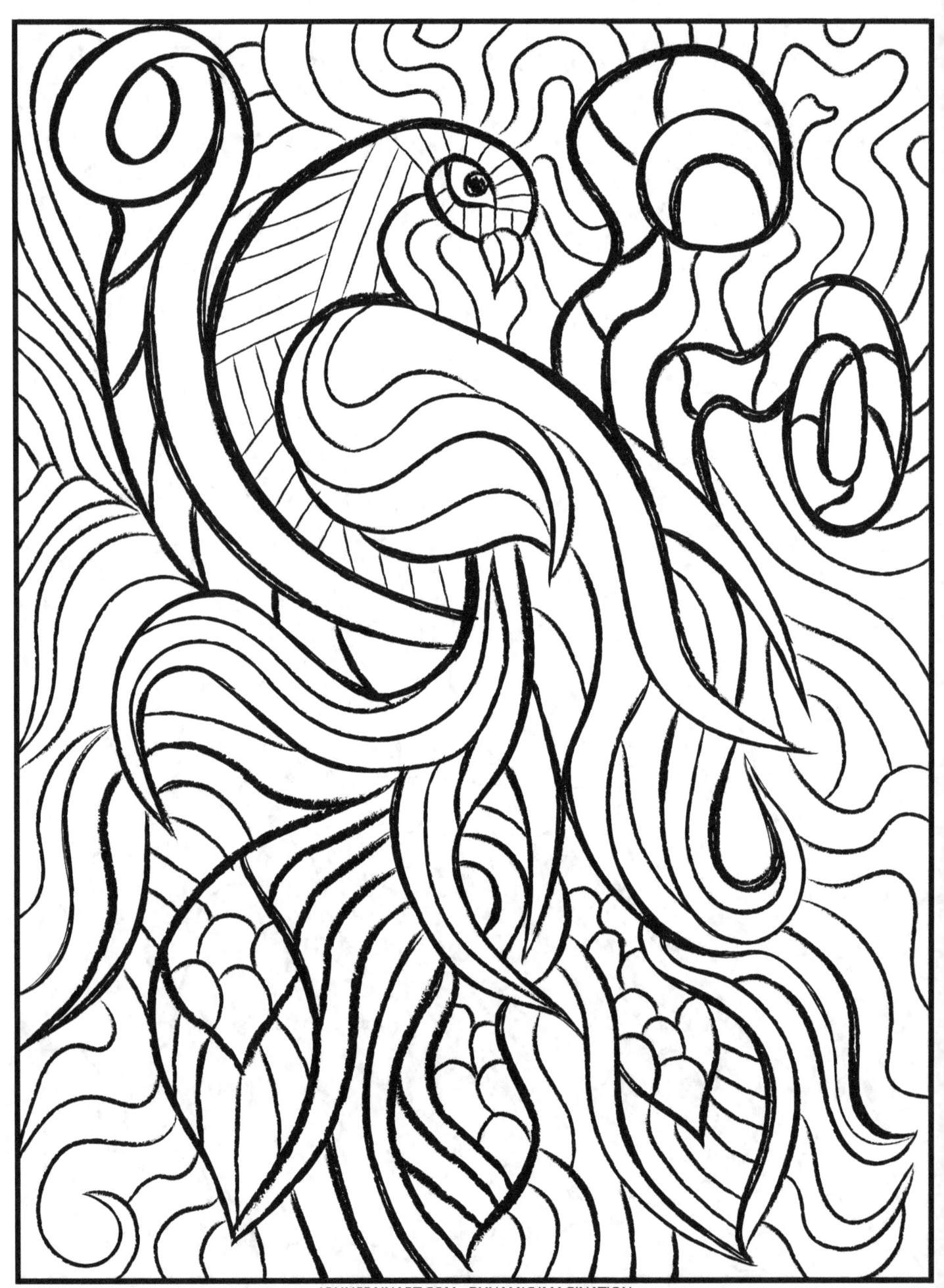

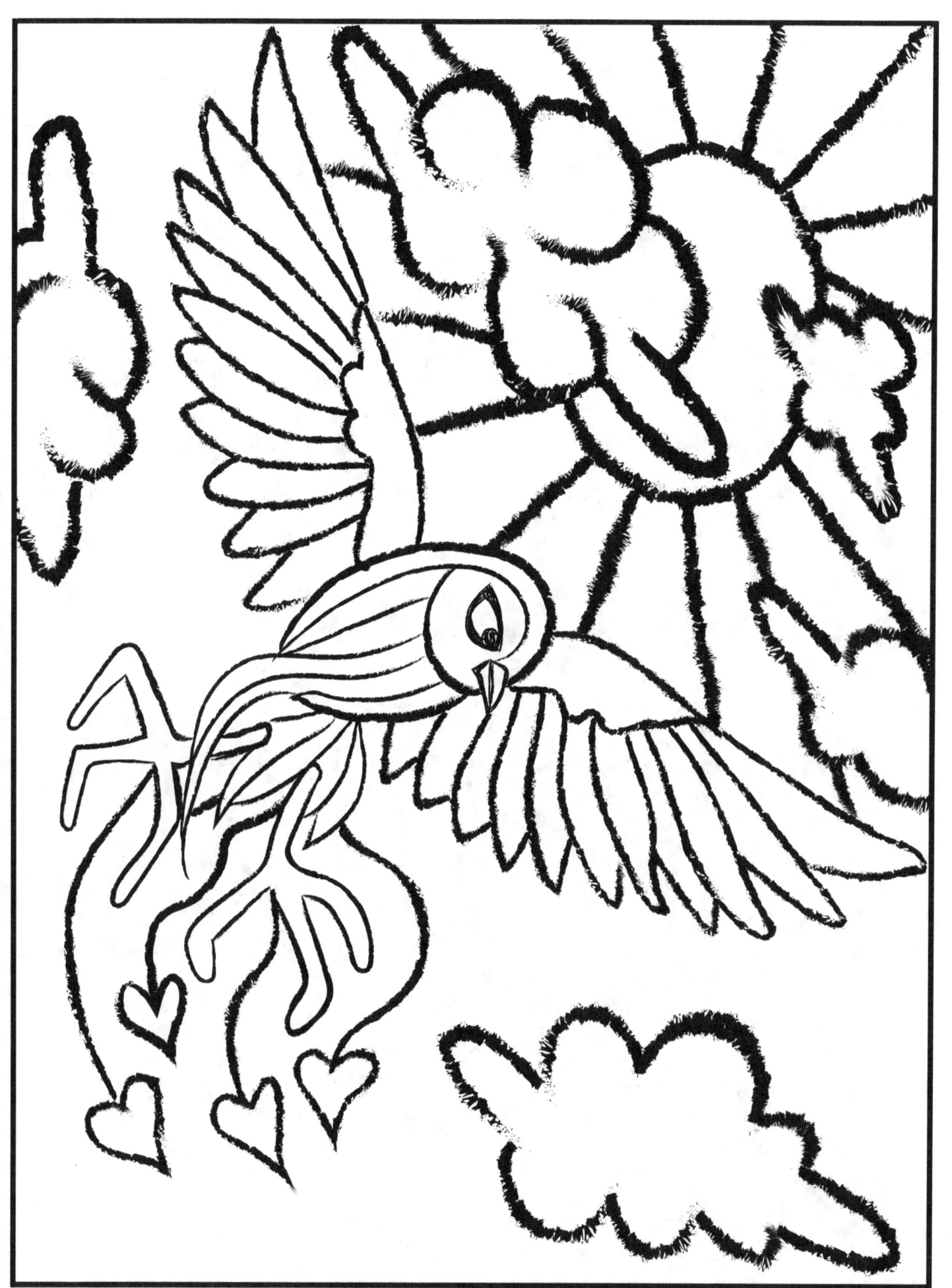

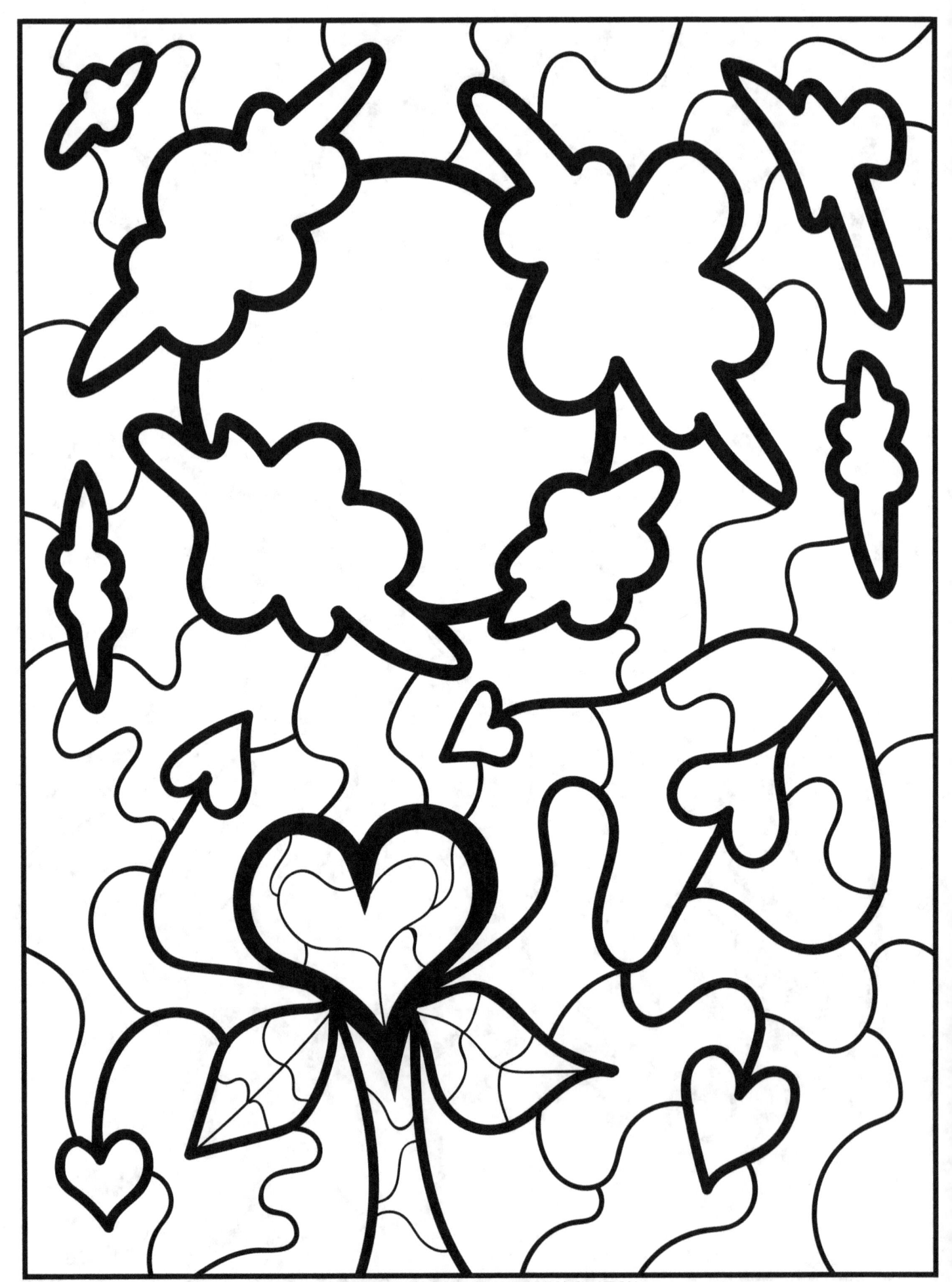

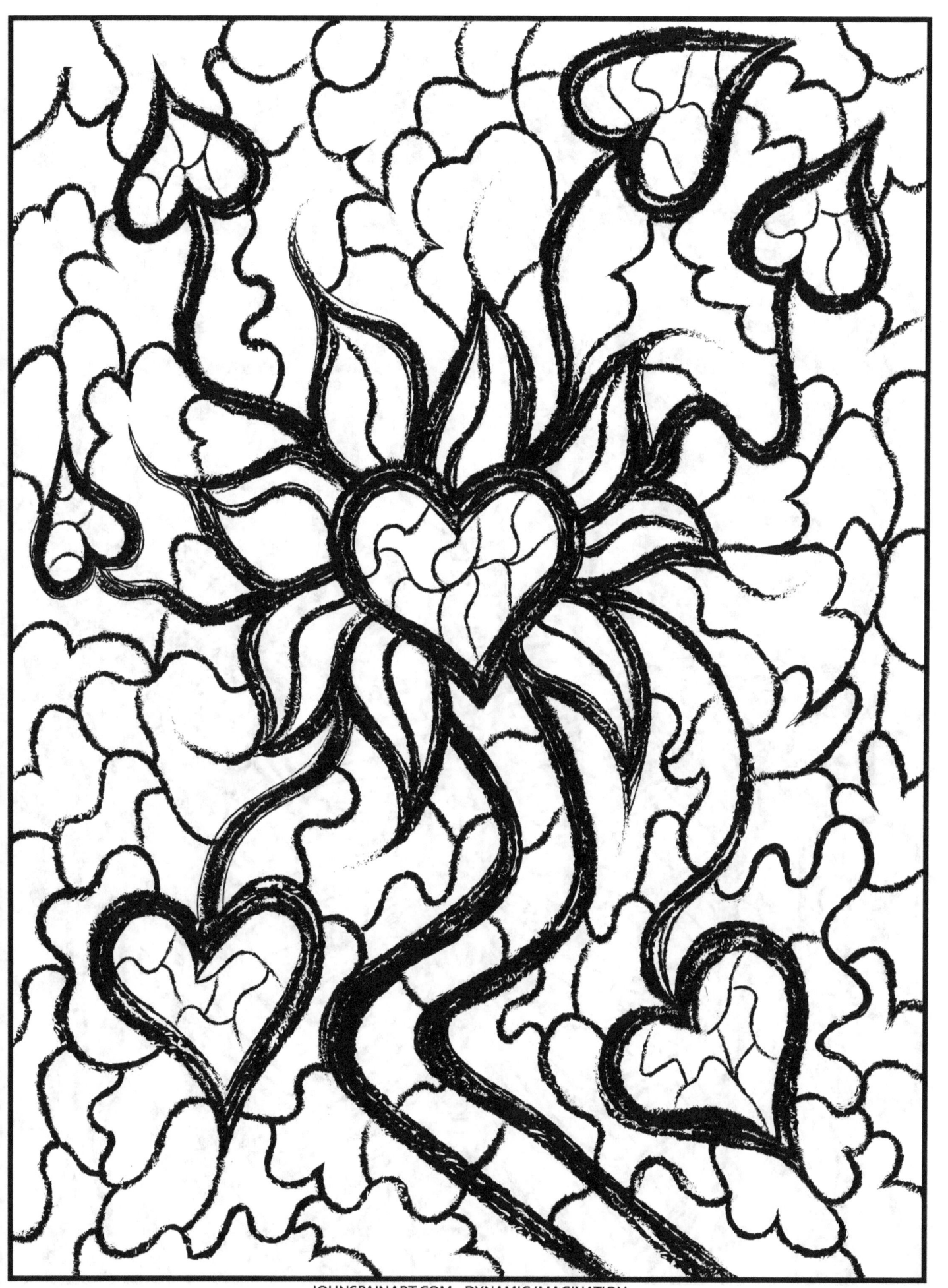

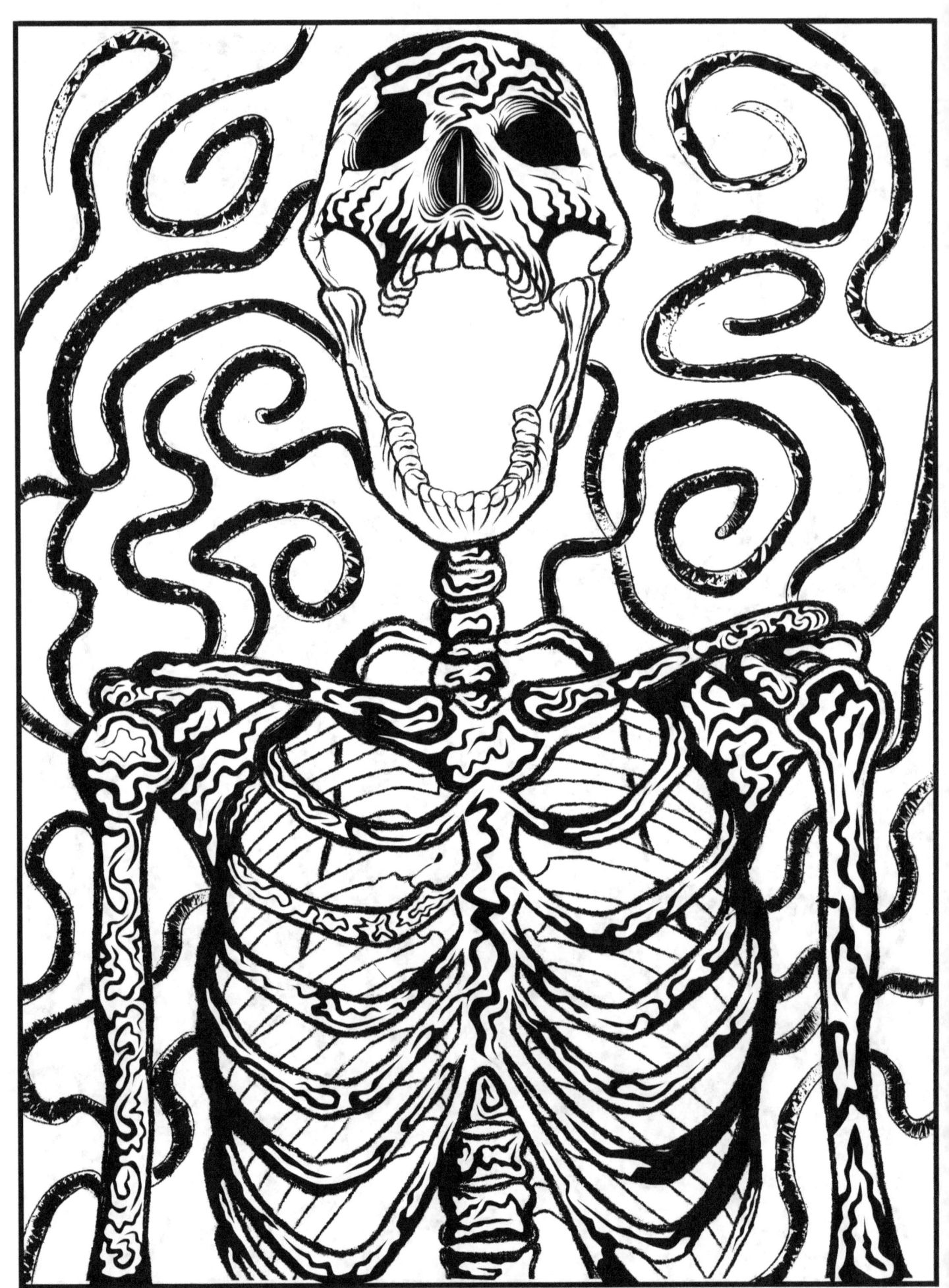

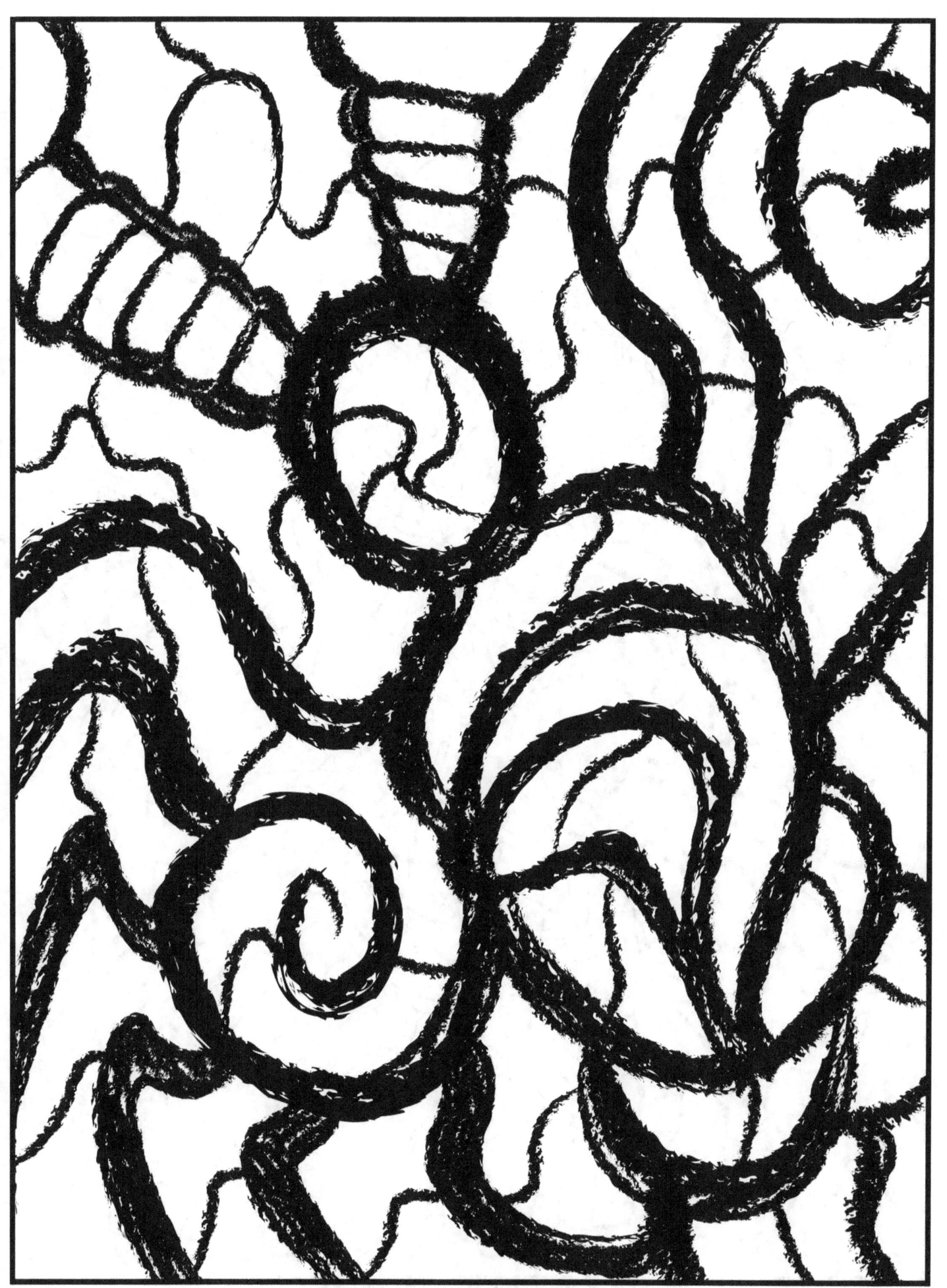

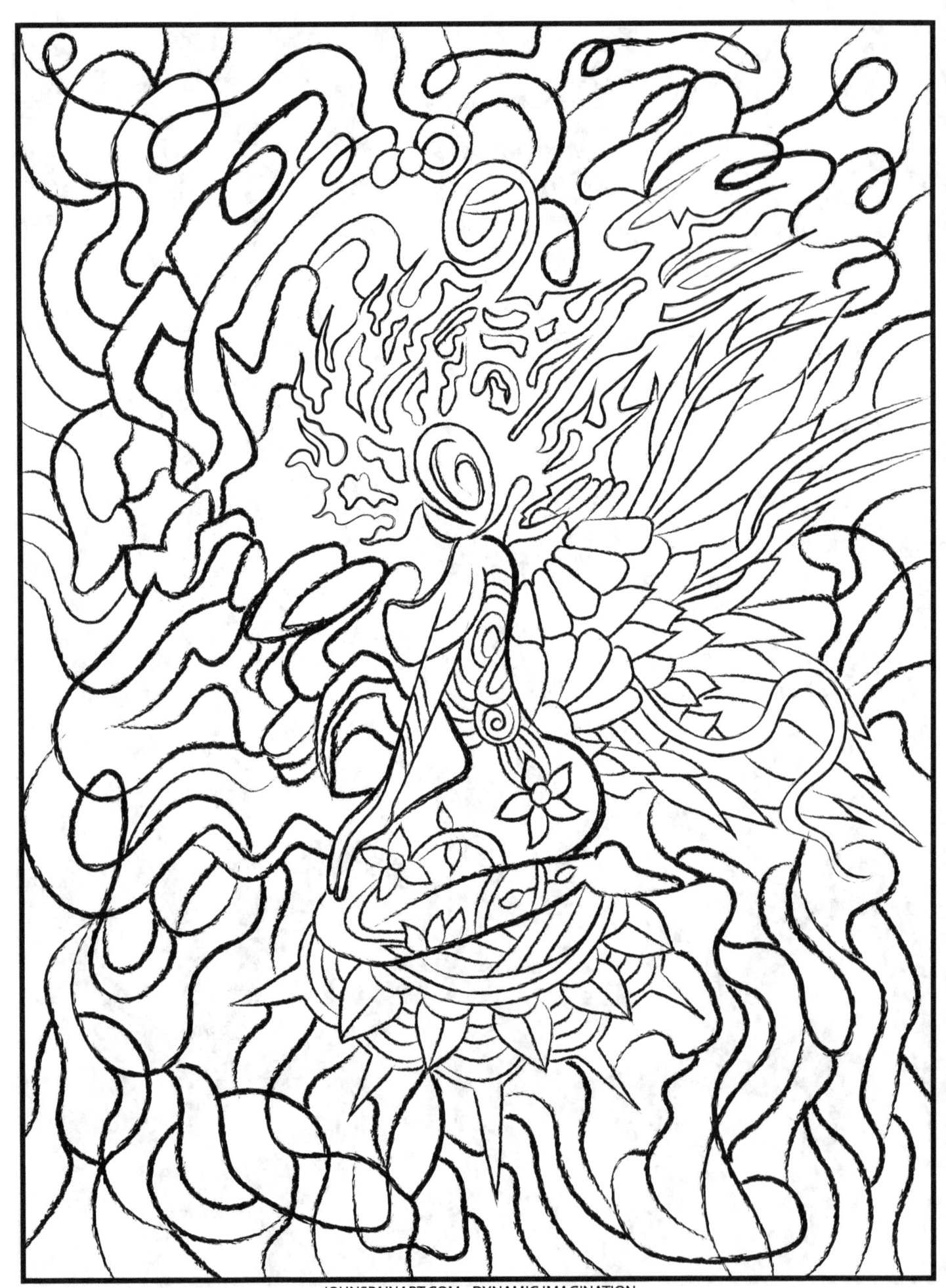

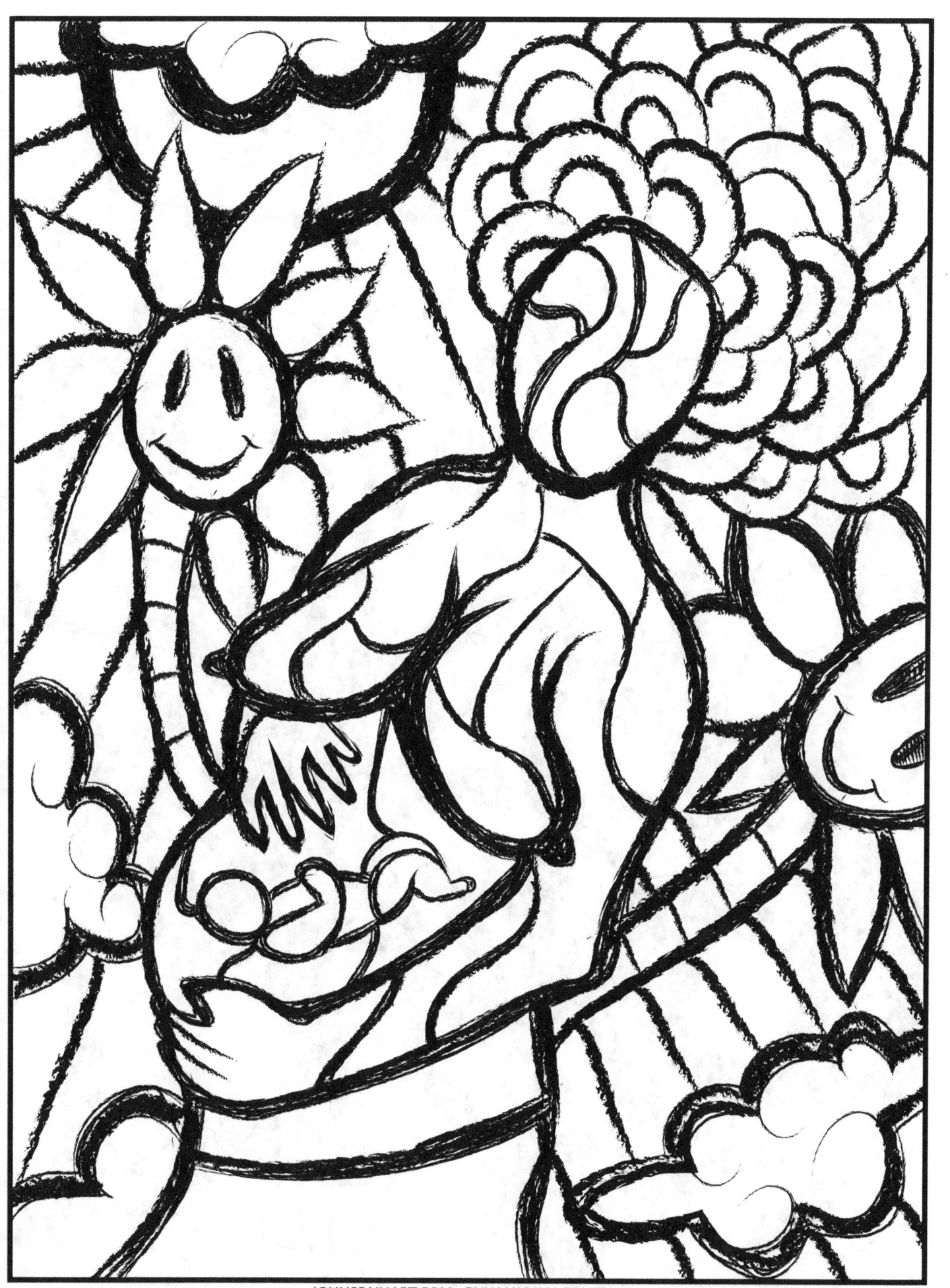

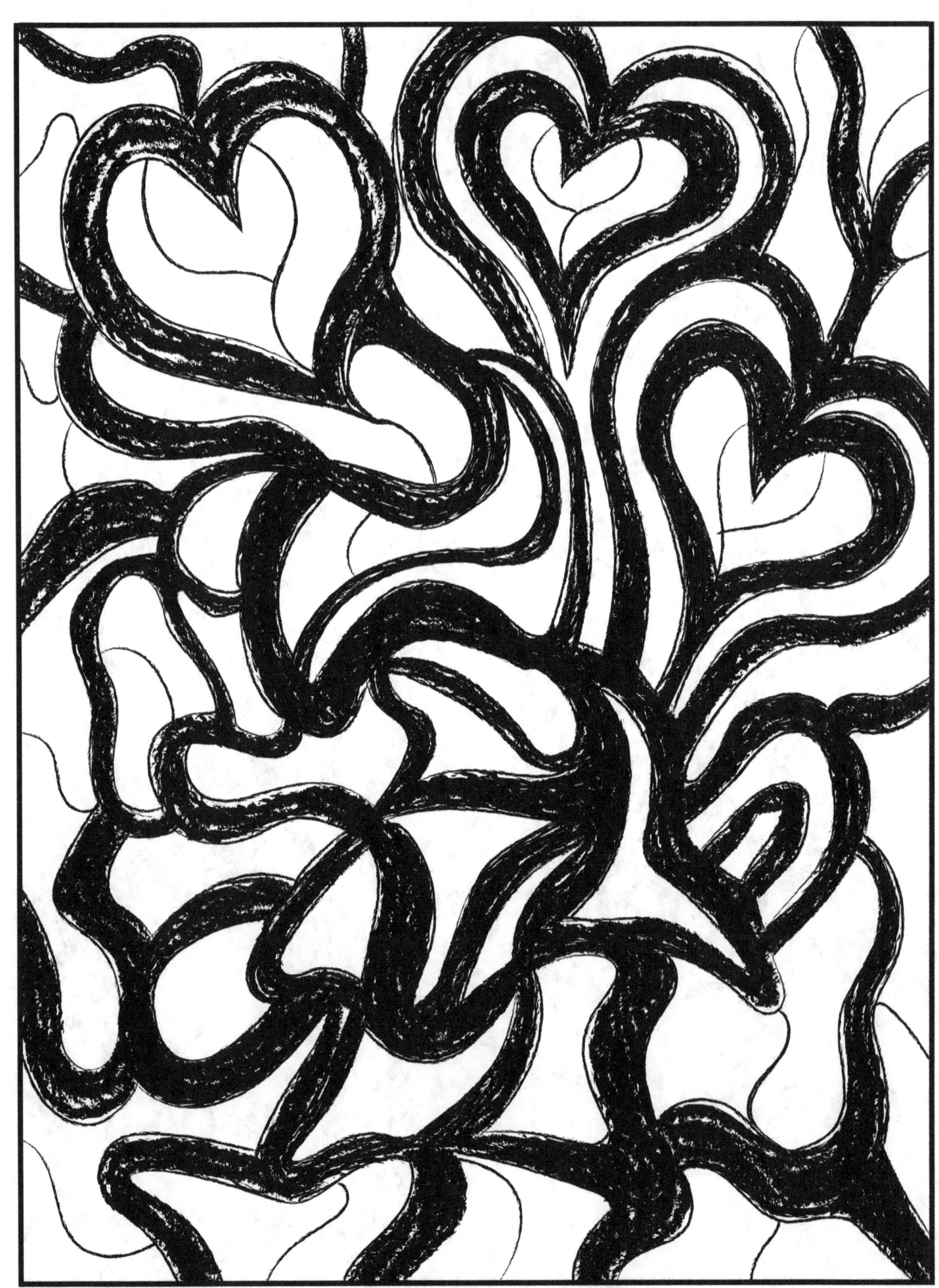

JOHNSPAINART.COM - DYNAMIC IMAGINATION

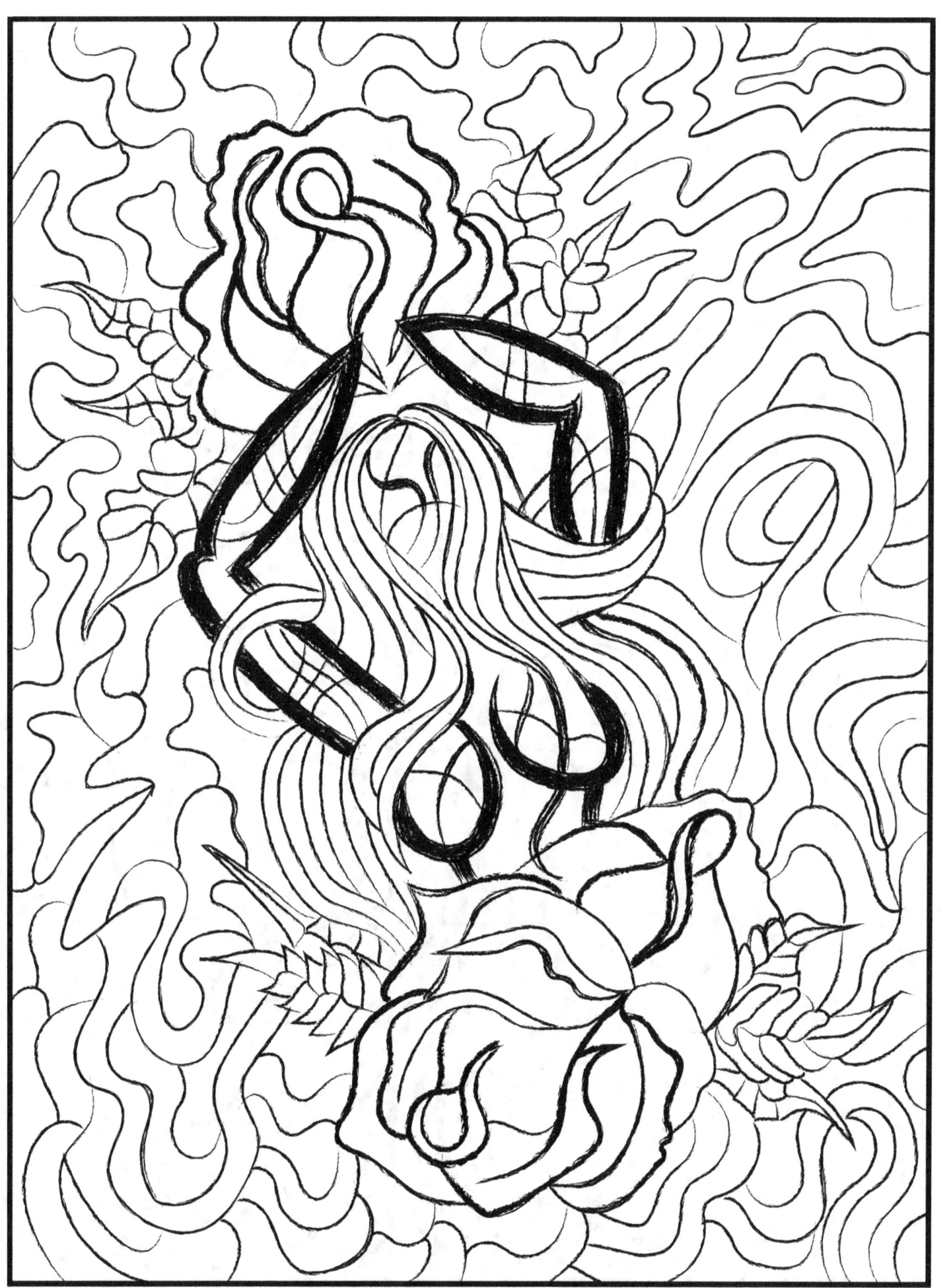

JOHNSPAINART.COM - DYNAMIC IMAGINATION

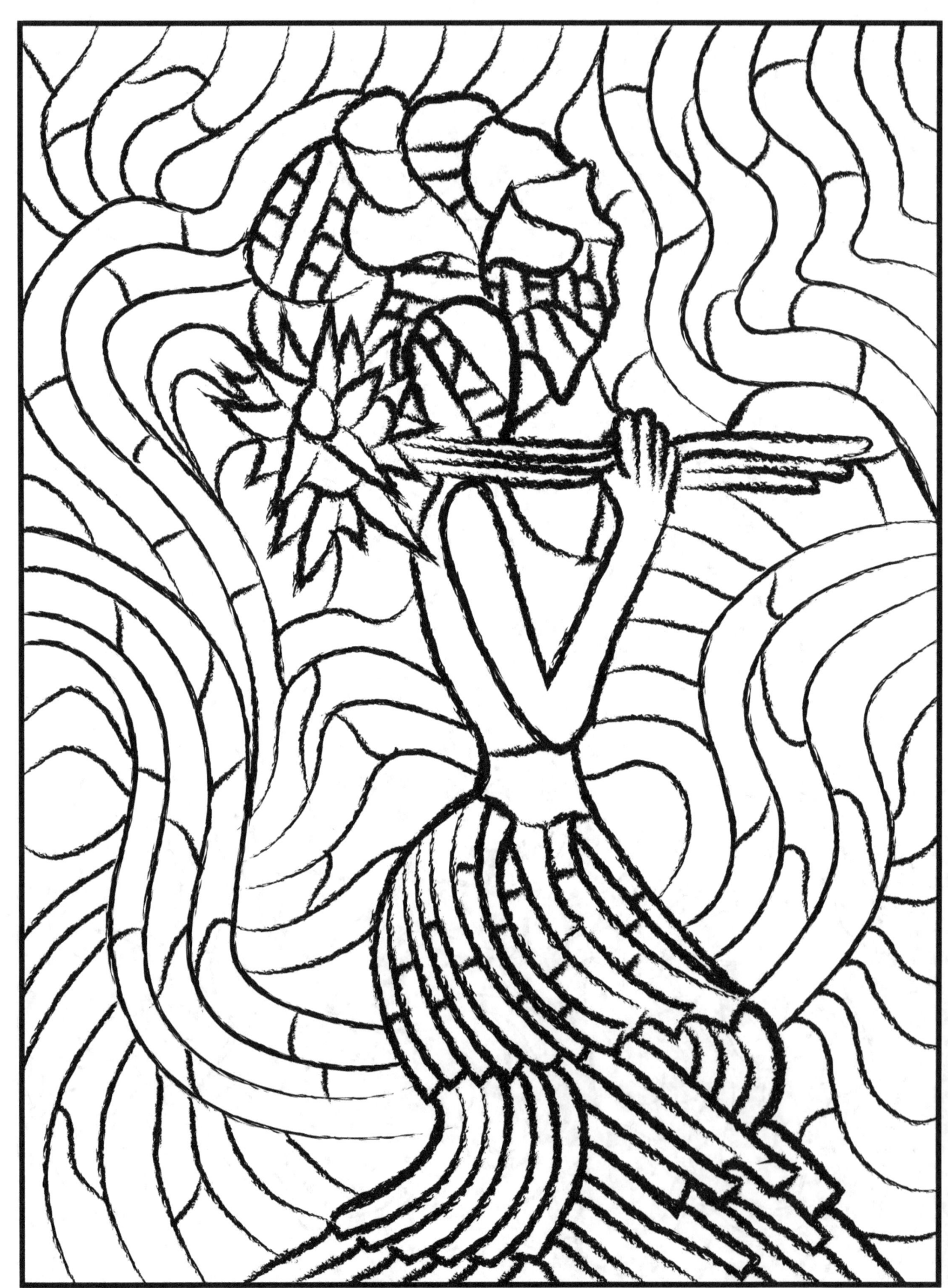

JOHNSPAINART.COM - DYNAMIC IMAGINATION

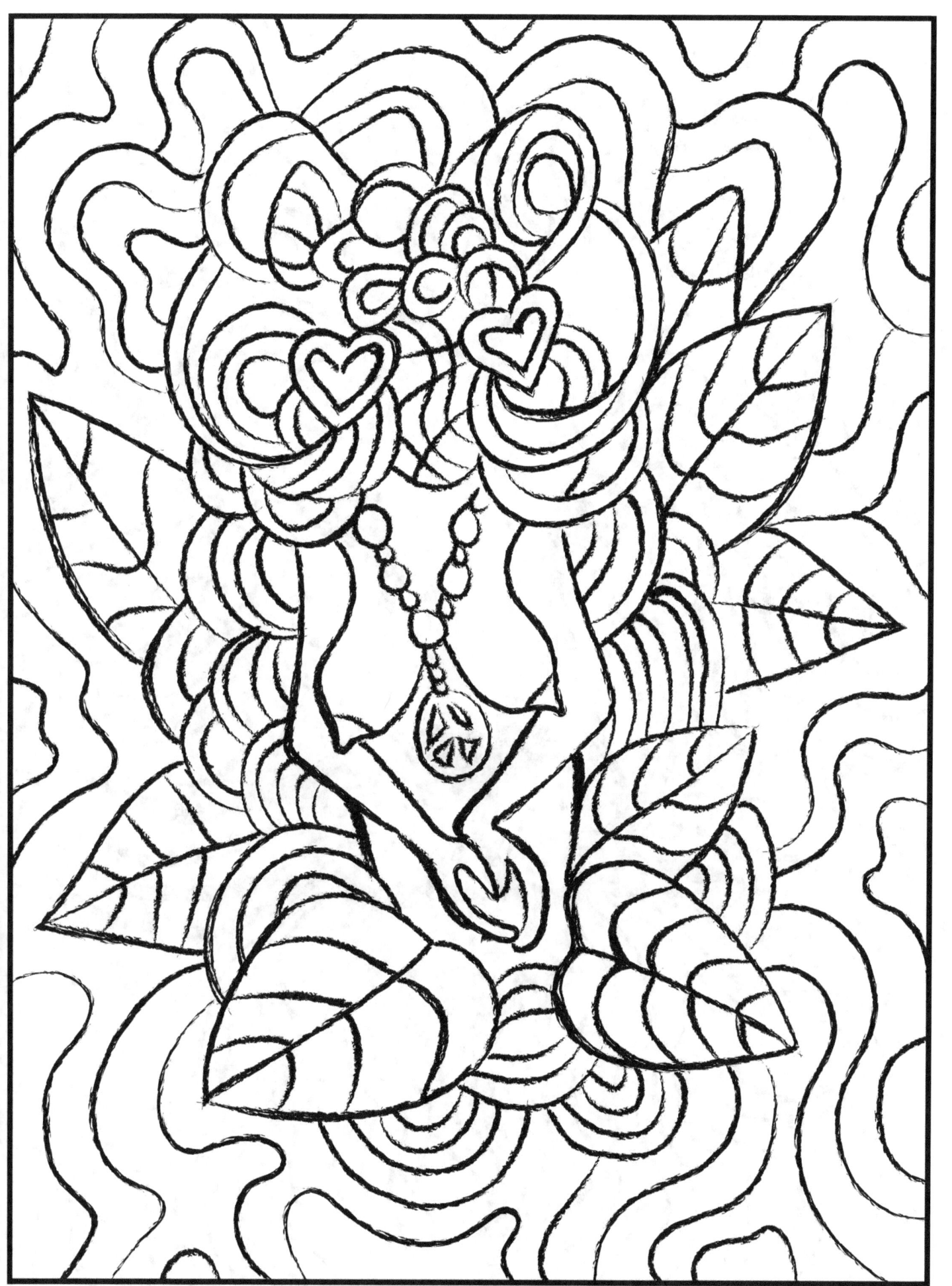
JOHNSPAINART.COM - DYNAMIC IMAGINATION

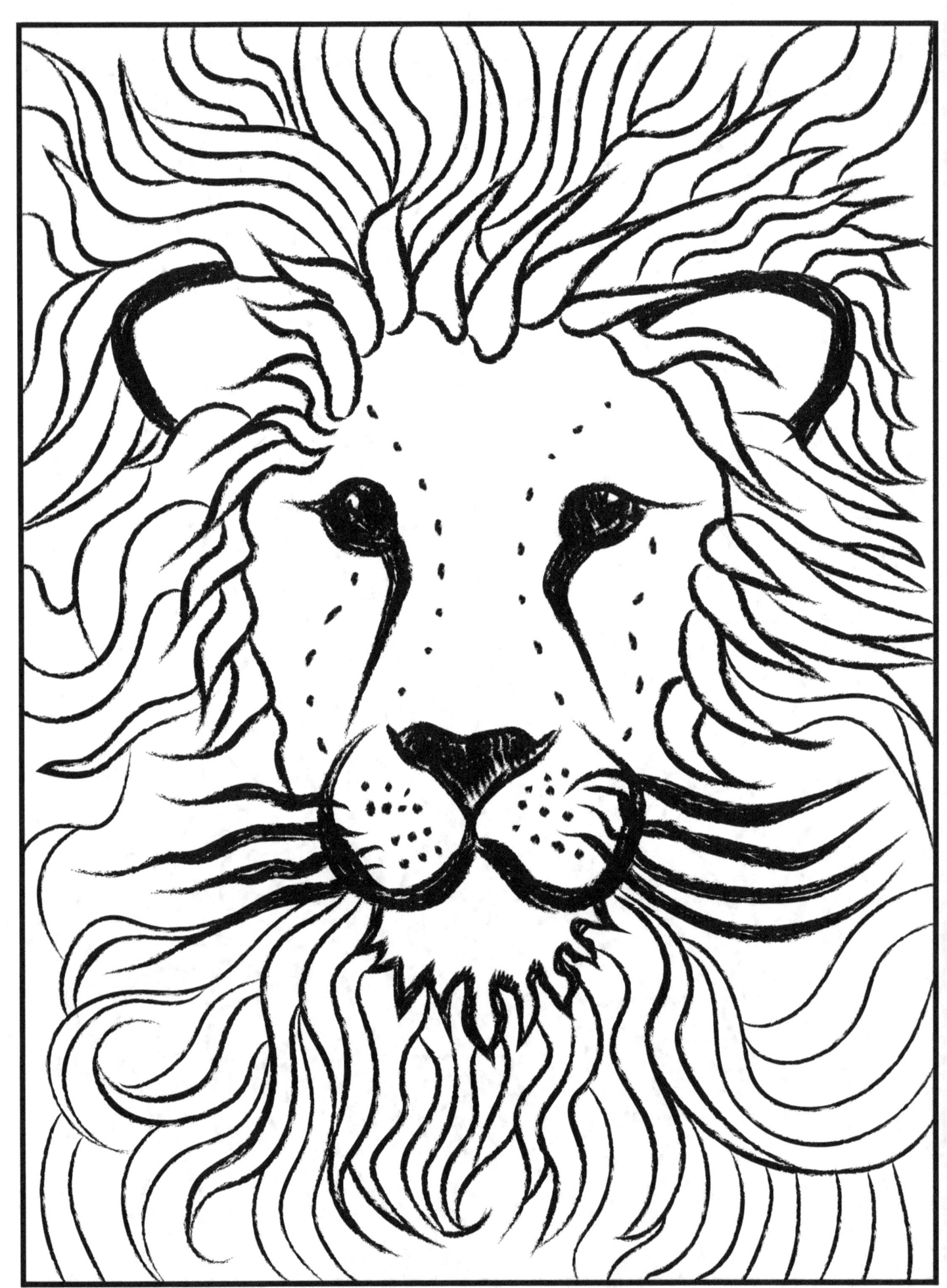
JOHNSPAINART.COM - DYNAMIC IMAGINATION

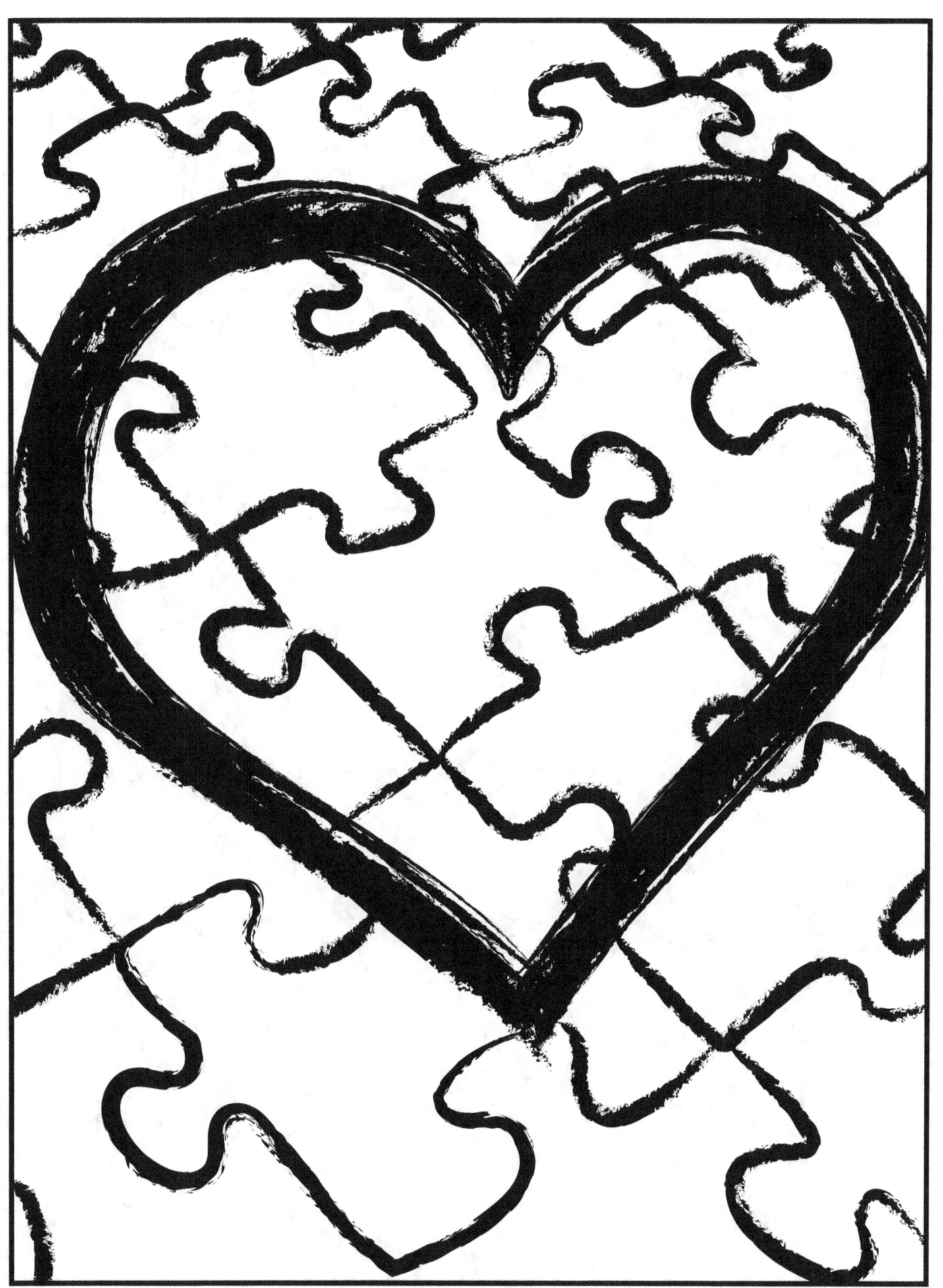

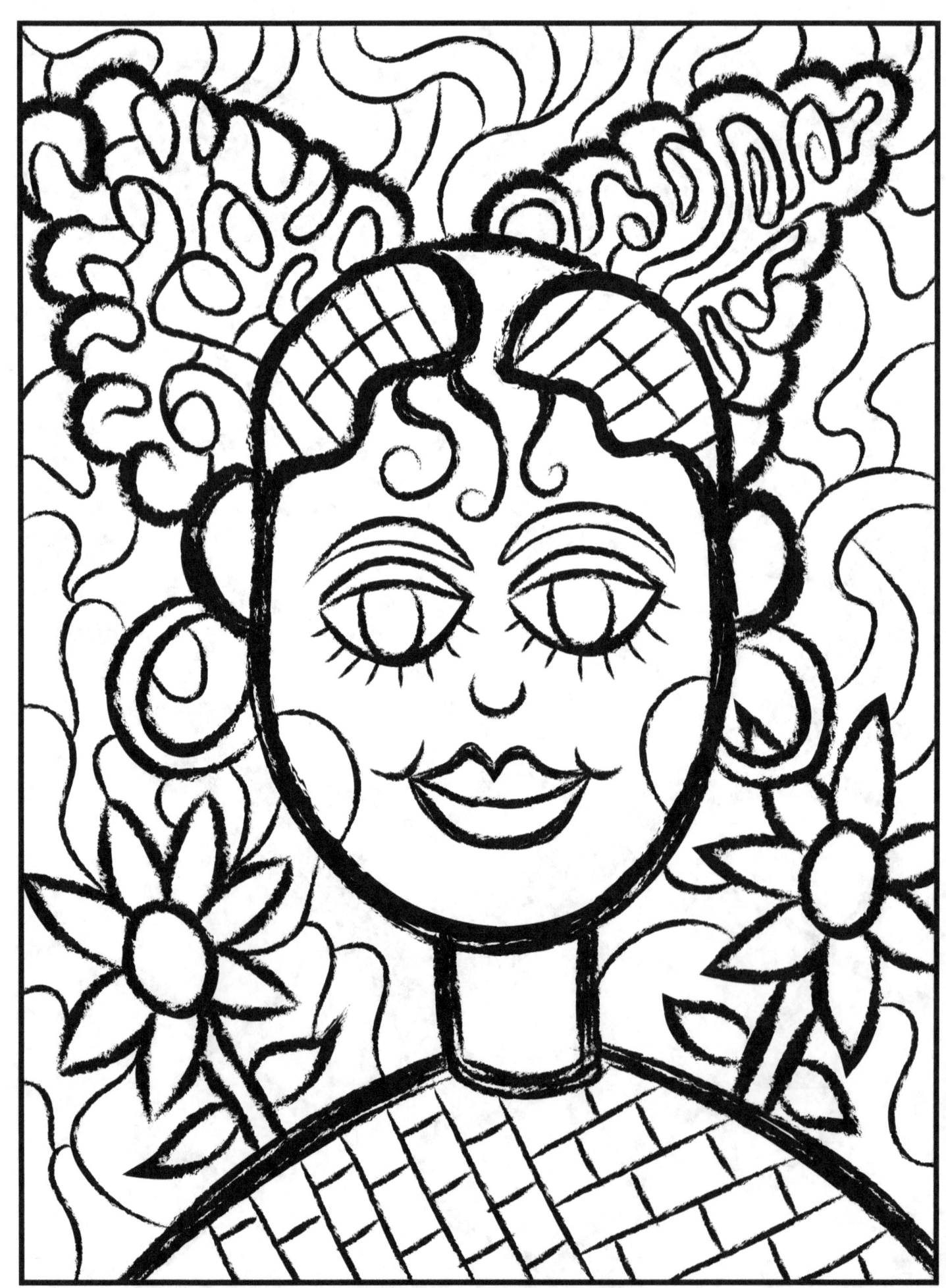

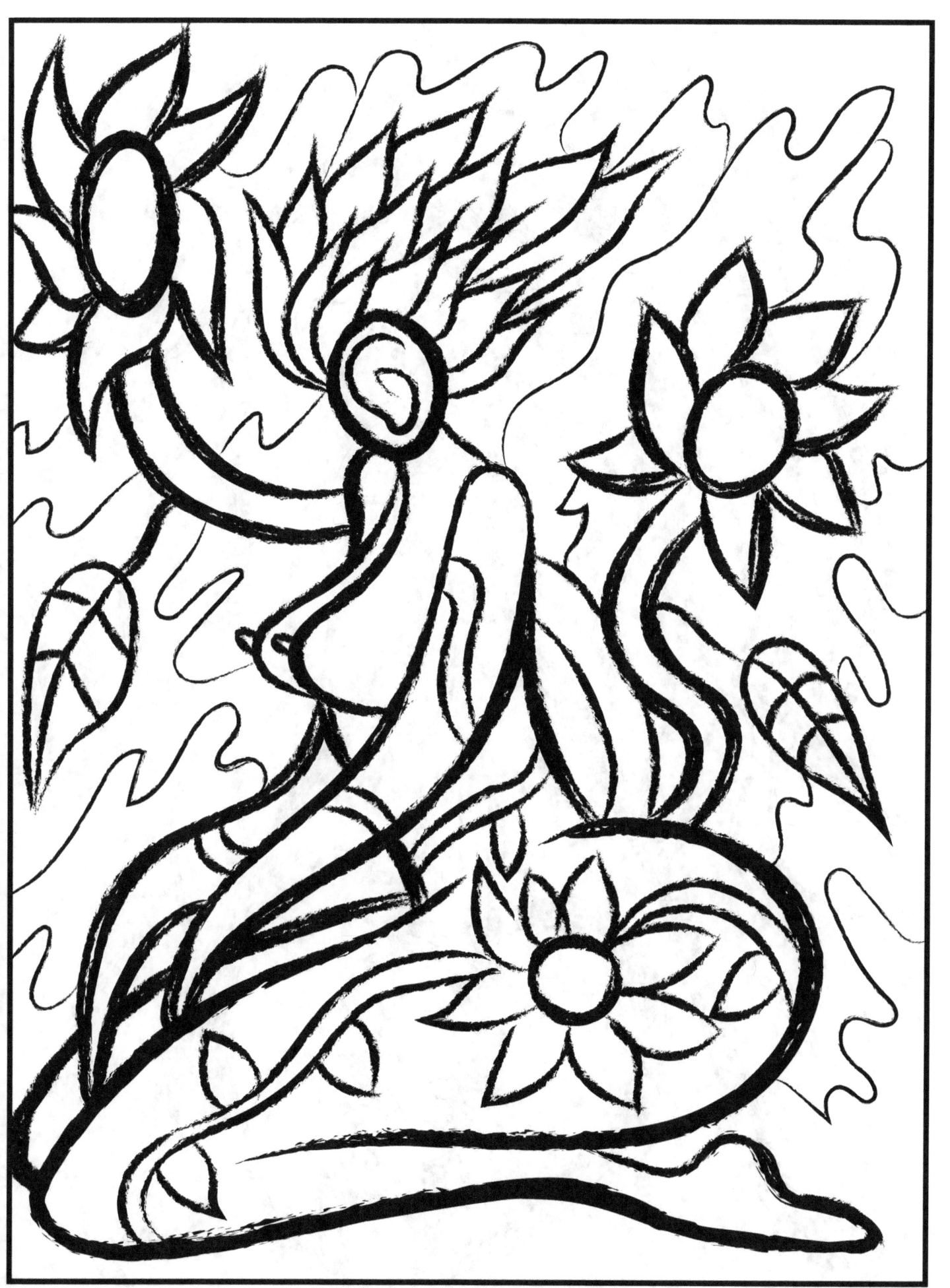

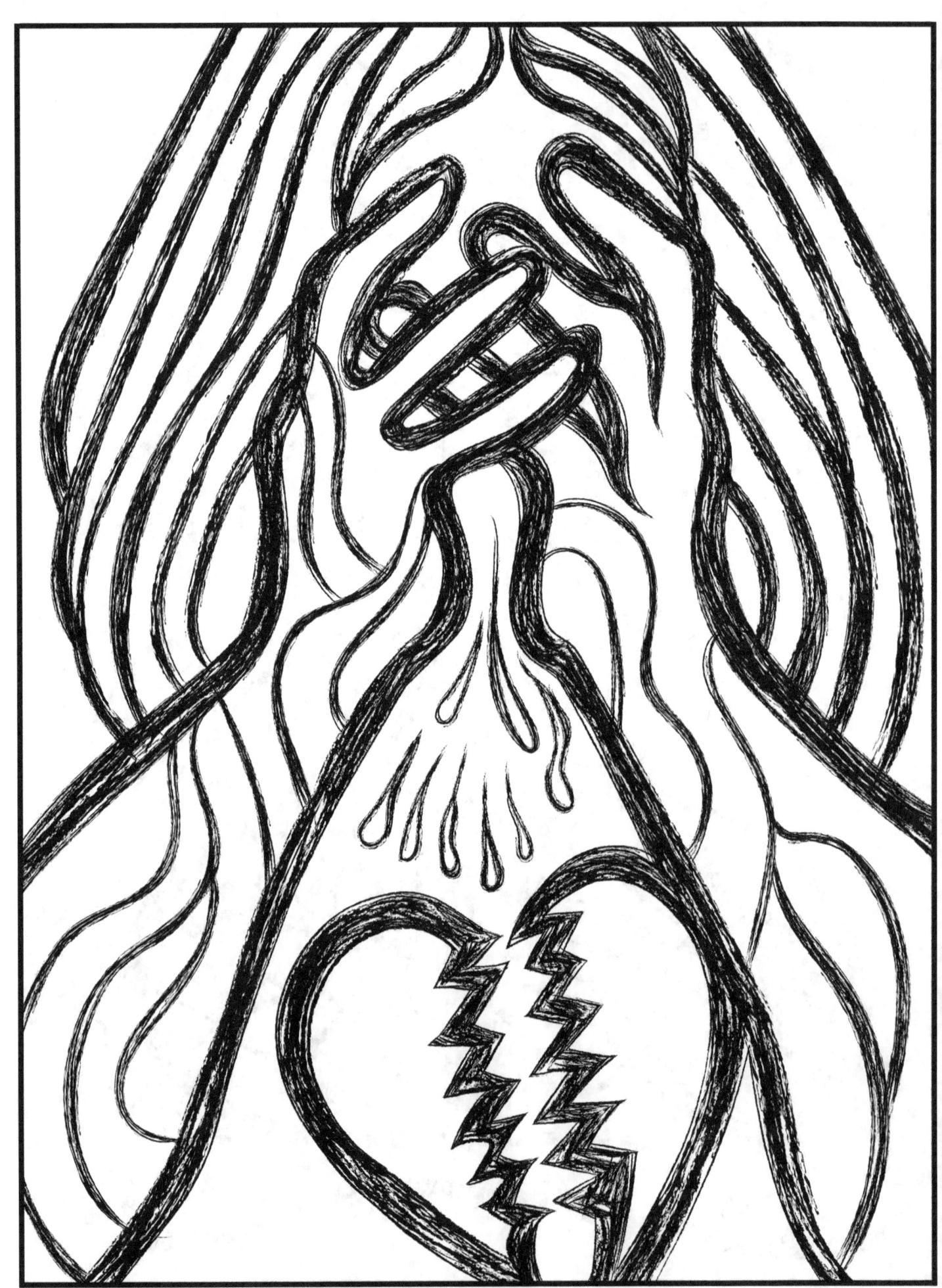

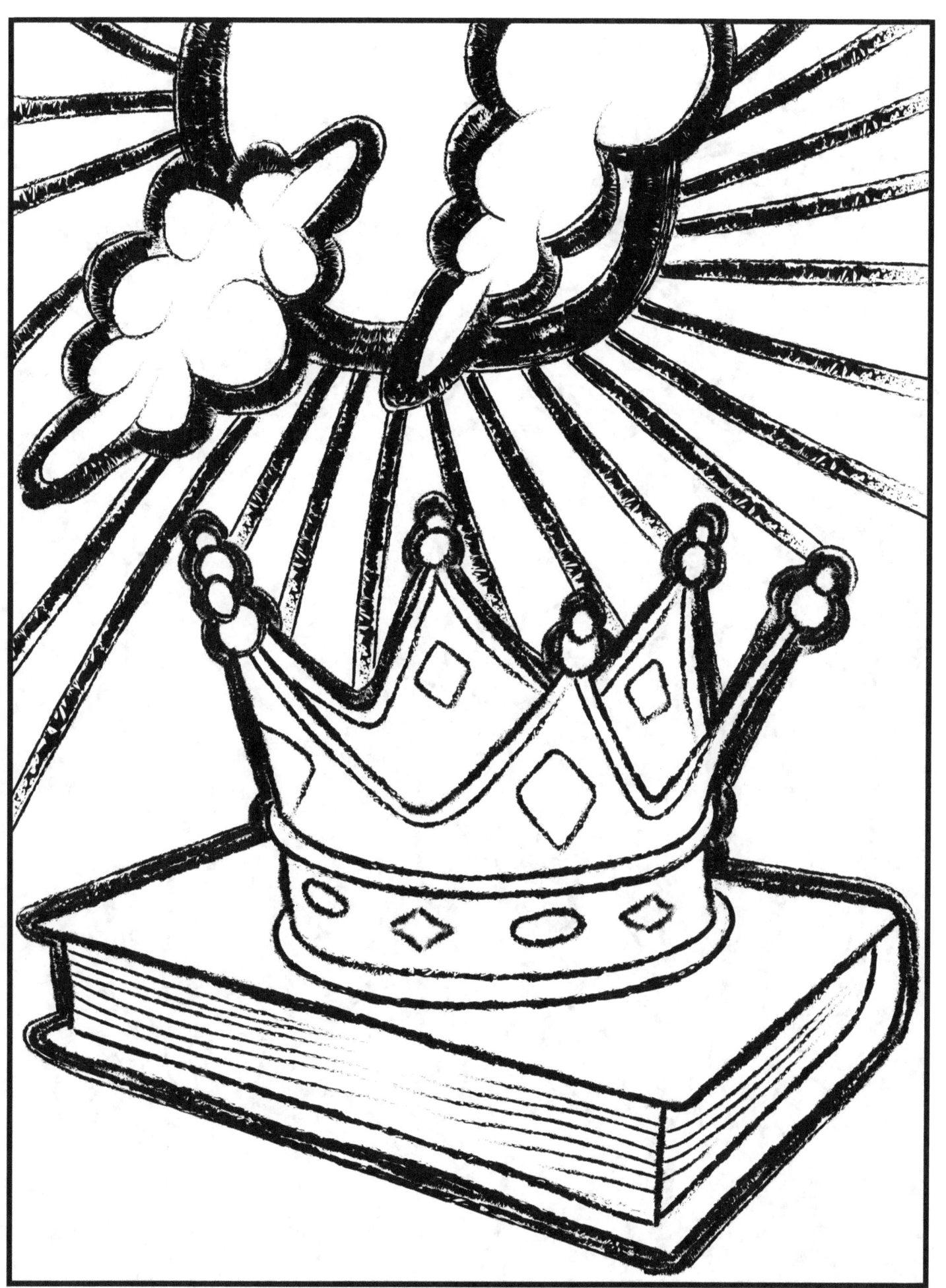

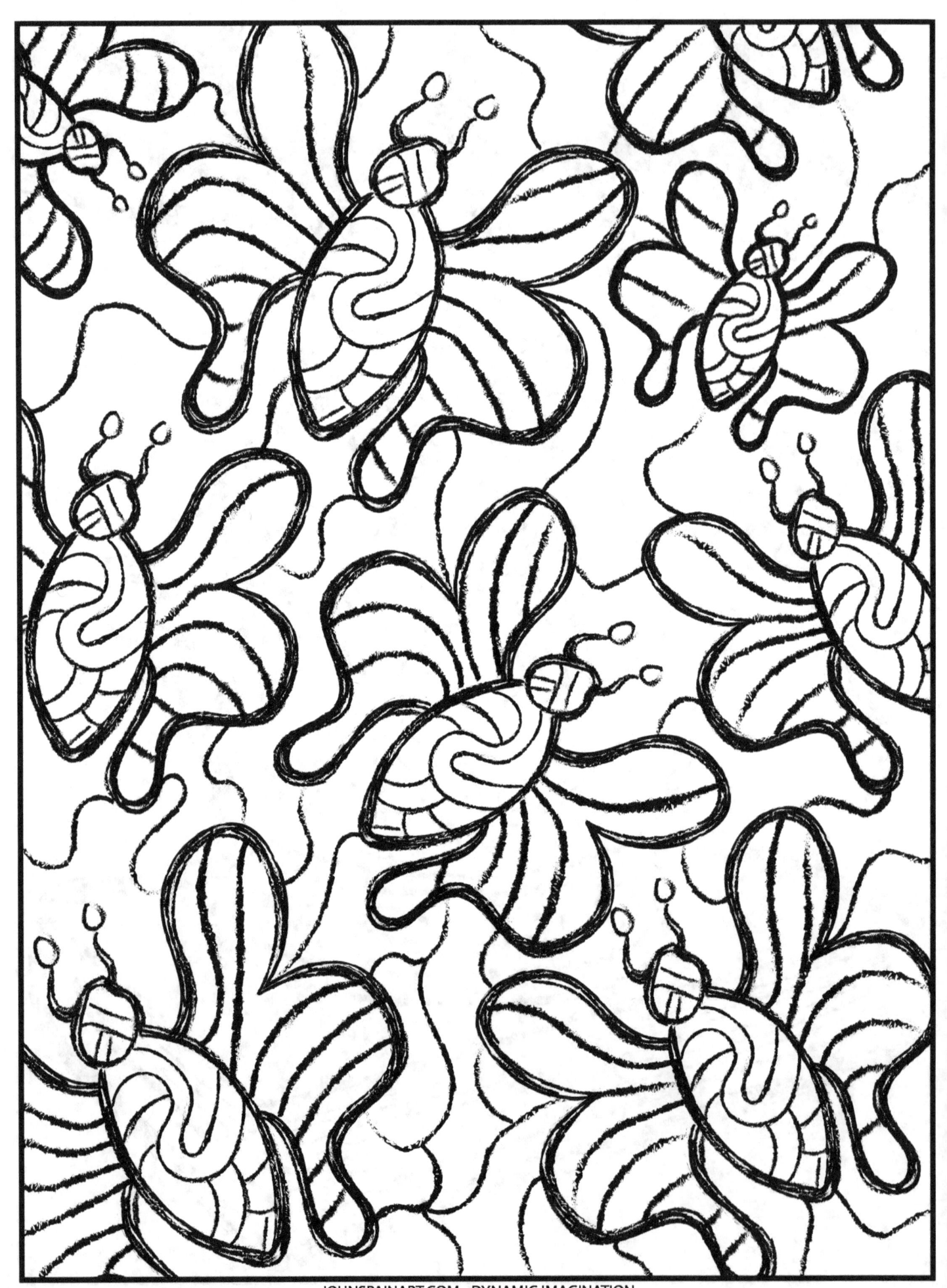

JOHNSPAINART.COM - DYNAMIC IMAGINATION

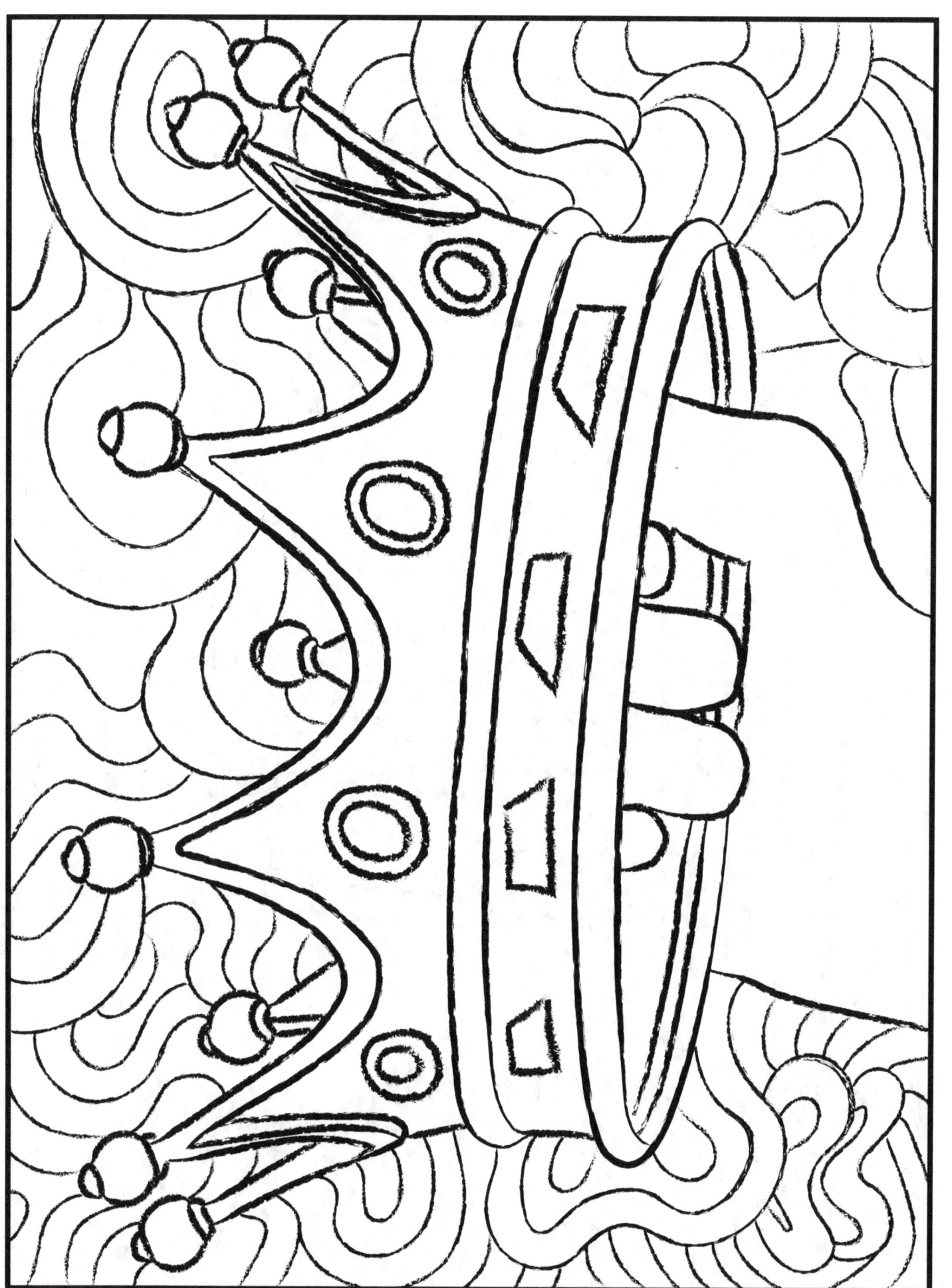

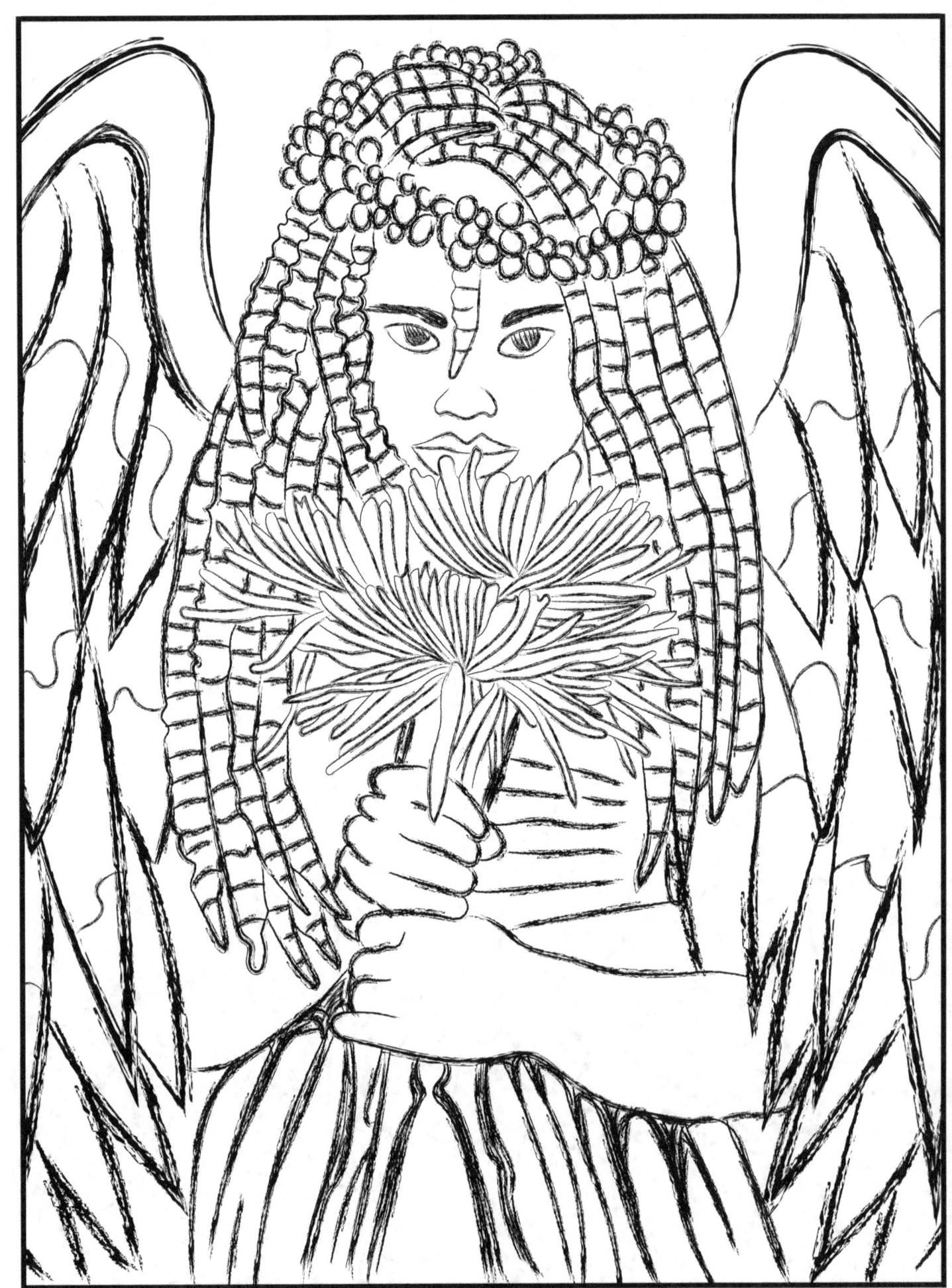

JOHNSPAINART.COM - DYNAMIC IMAGINATION

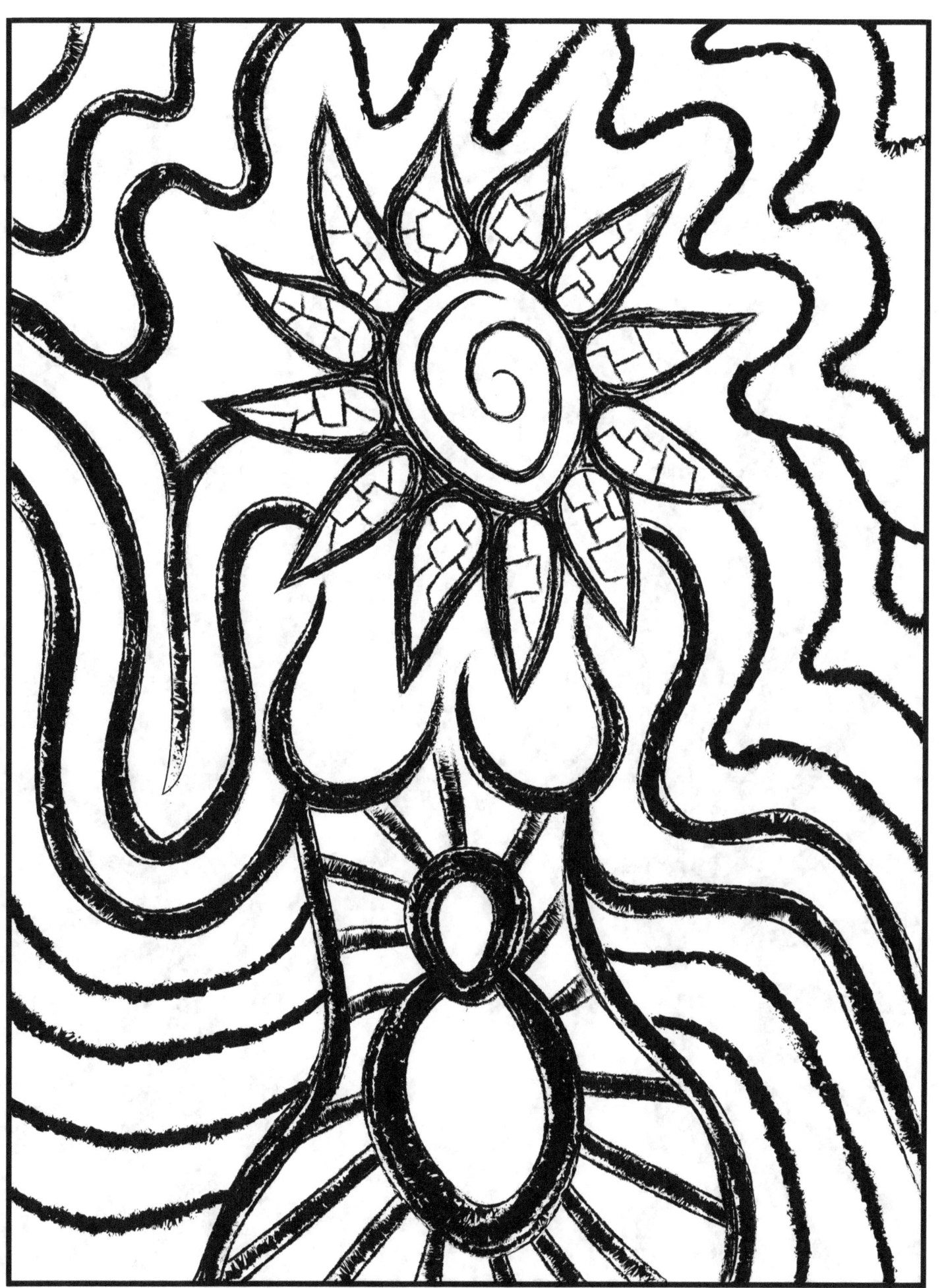

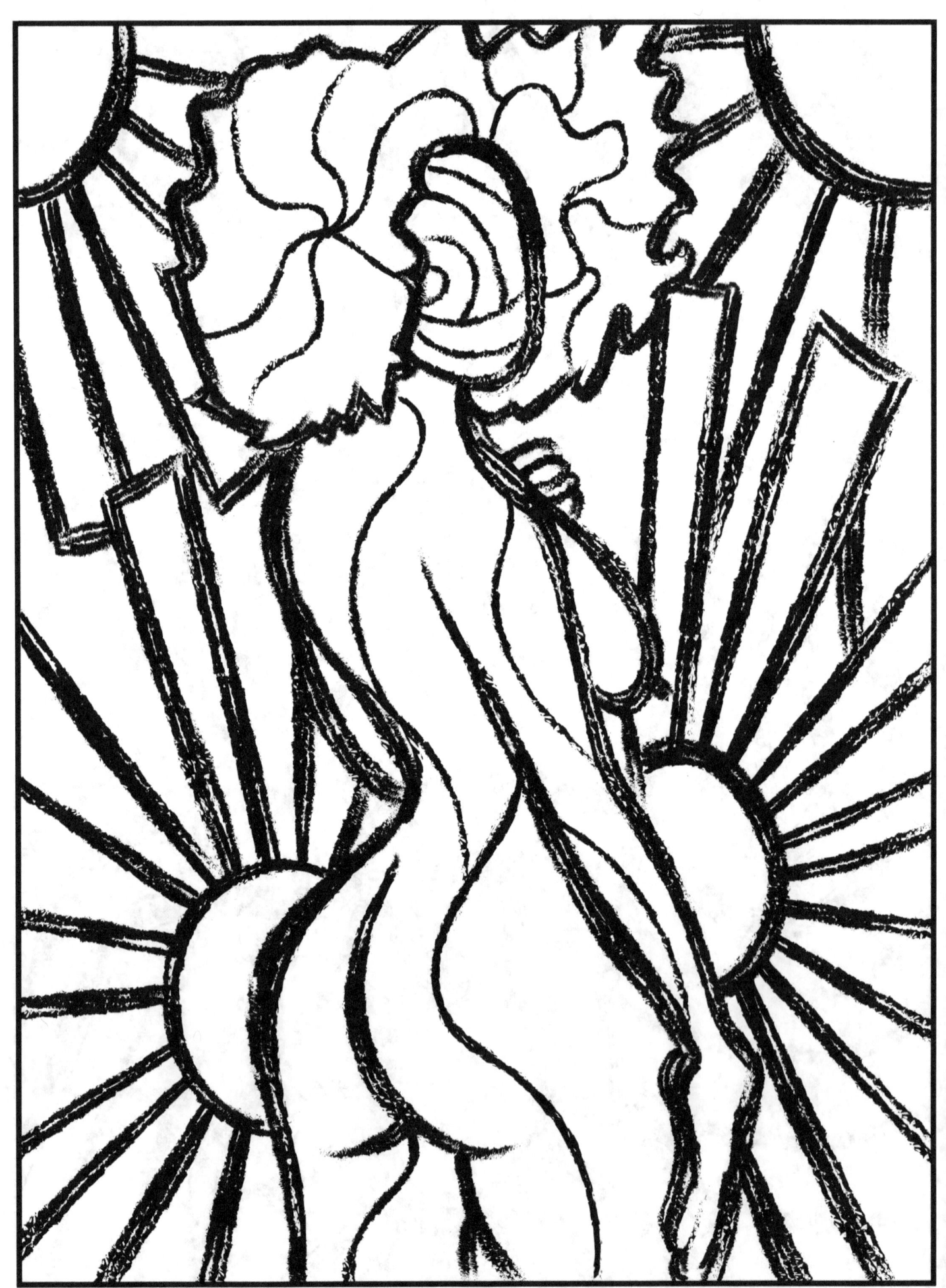

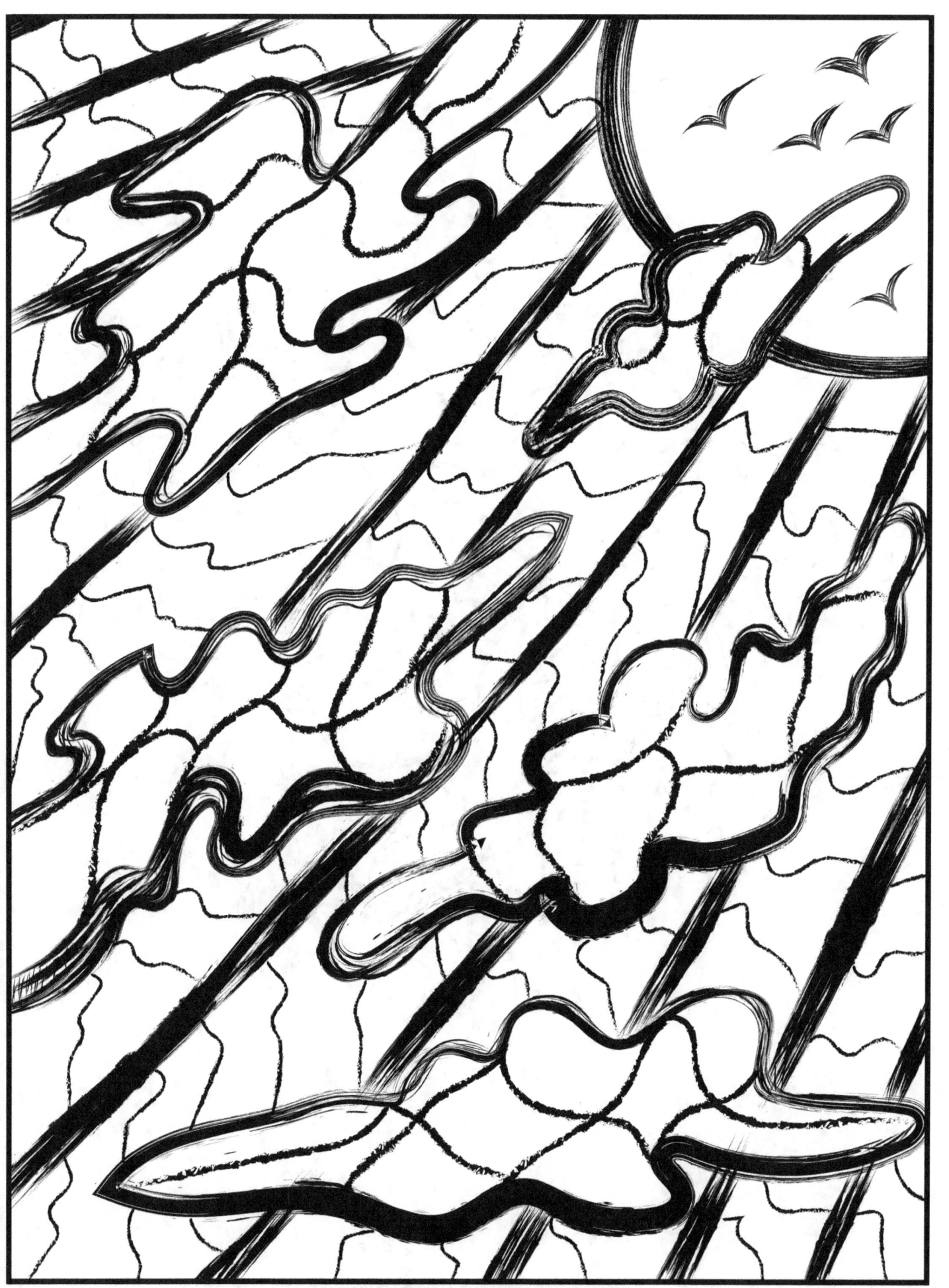

JOHNSPAINART.COM - DYNAMIC IMAGINATION

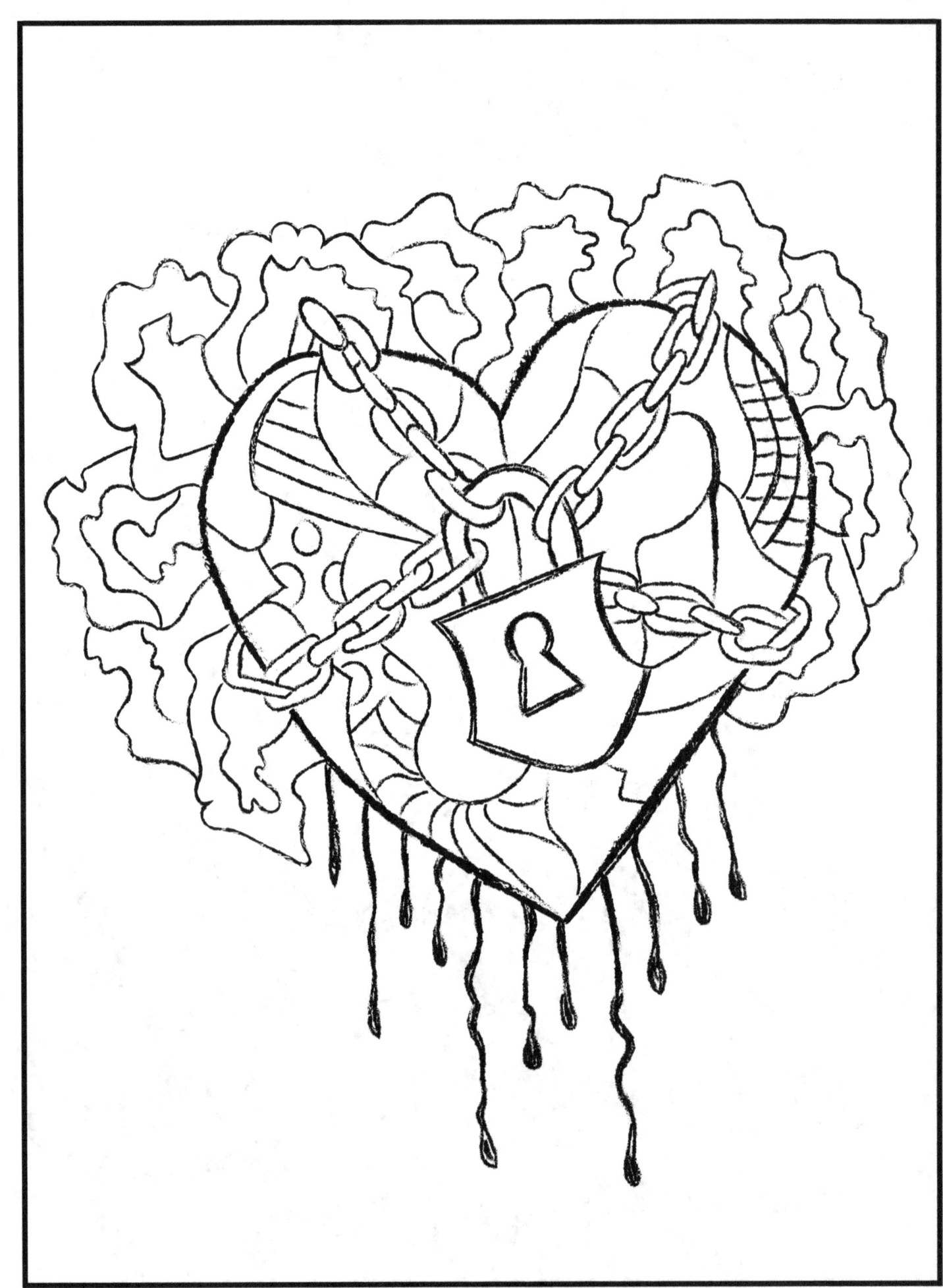

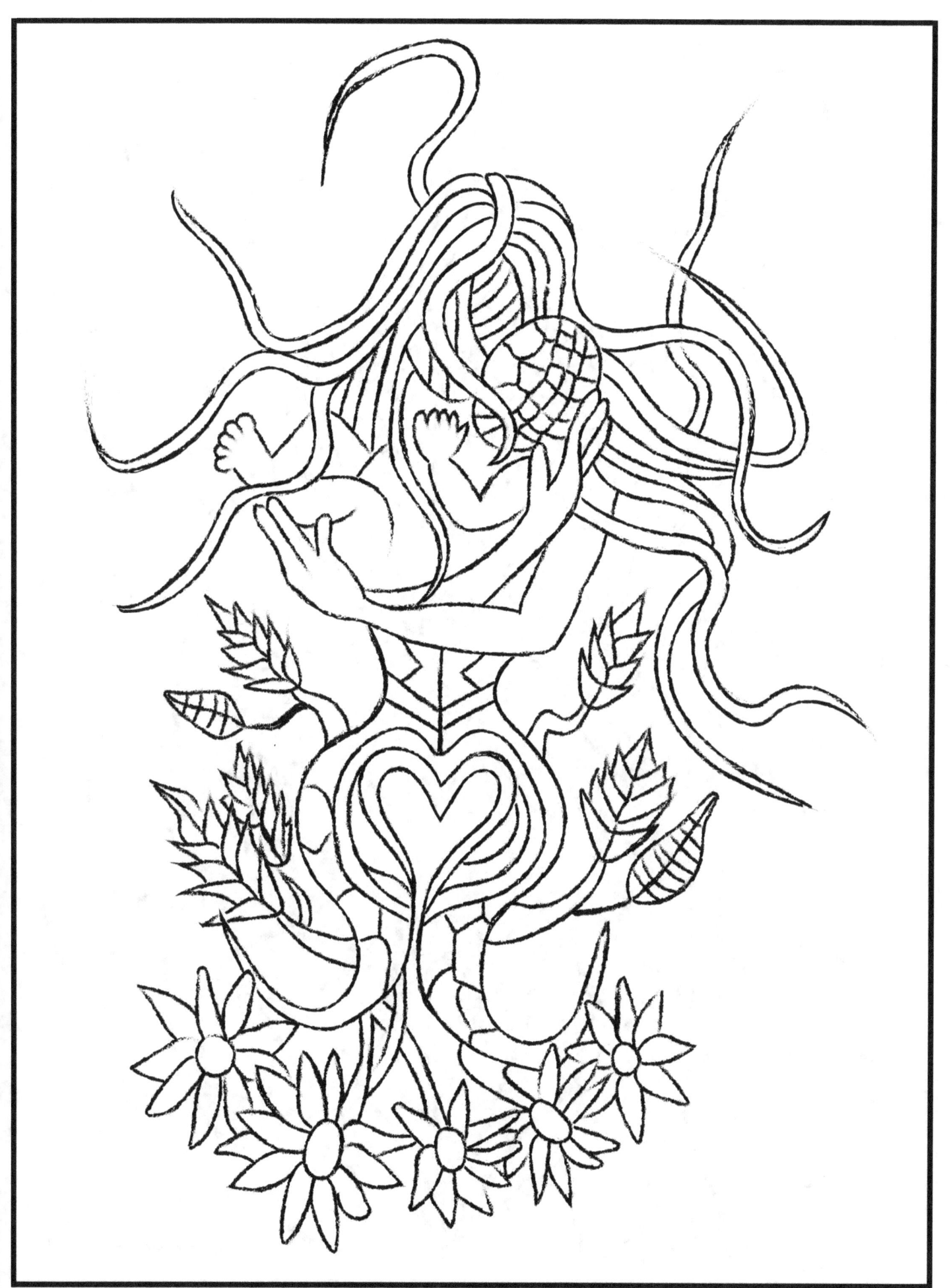

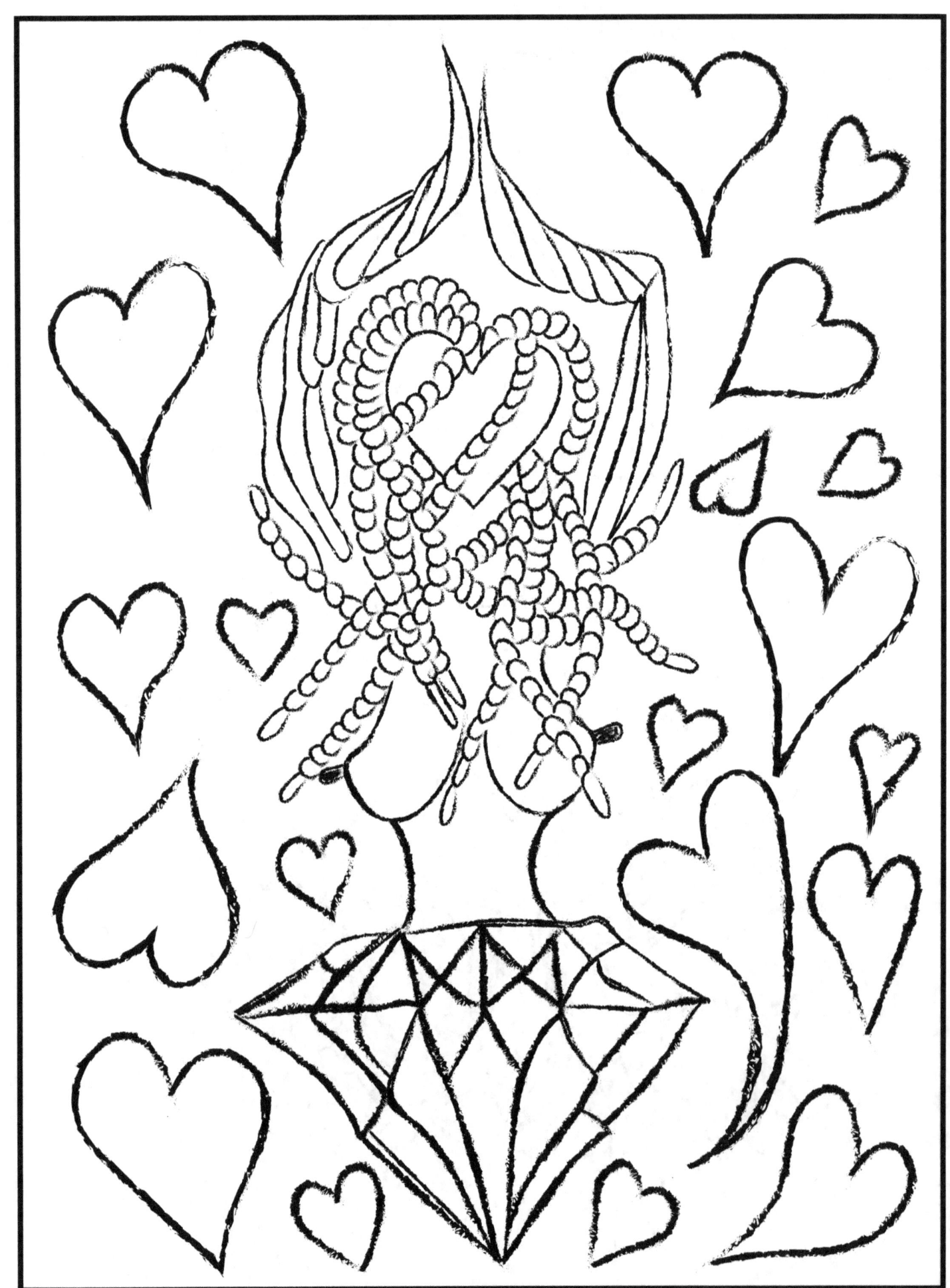

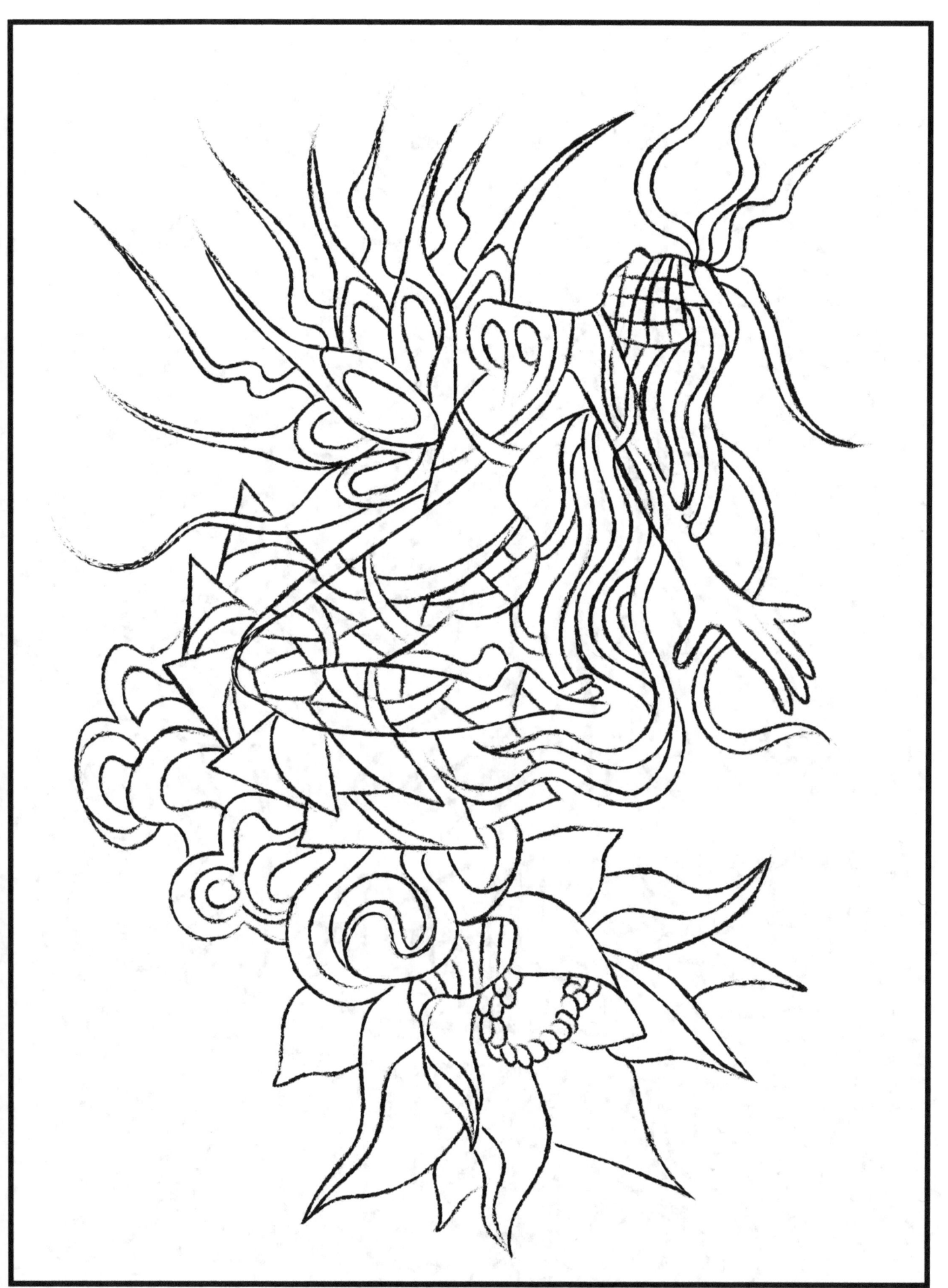

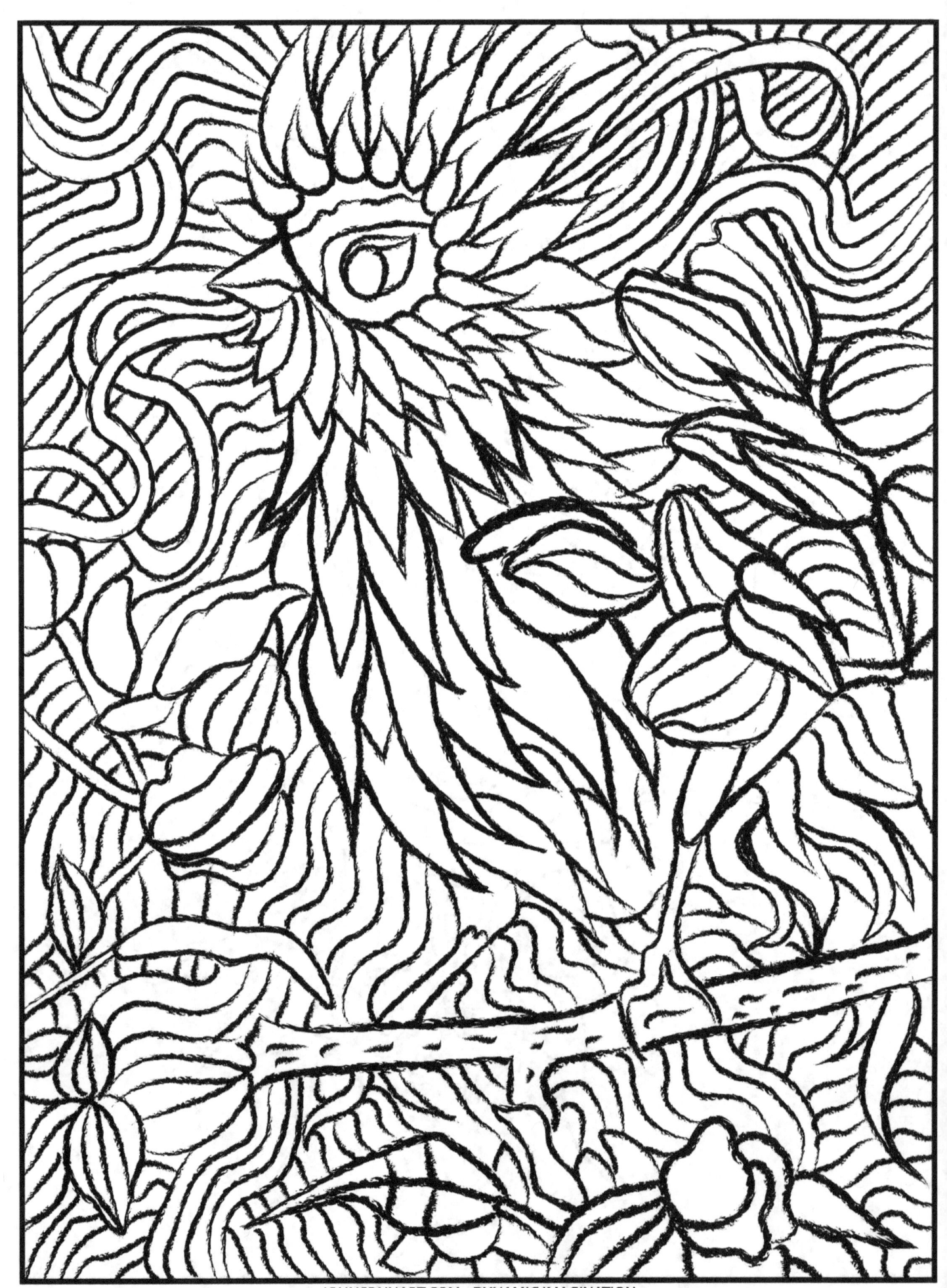

JOHNSPAINART.COM - DYNAMIC IMAGINATION

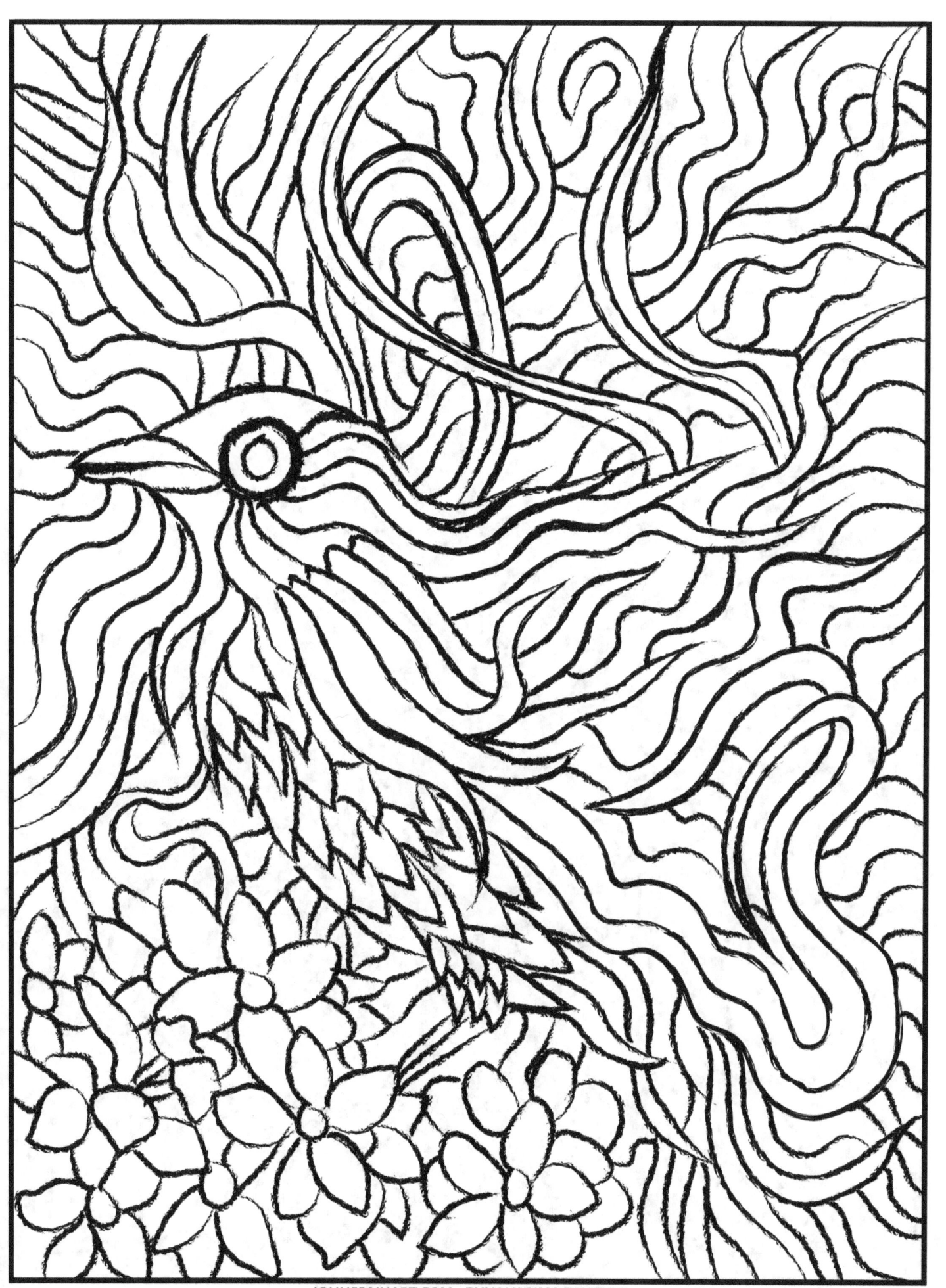

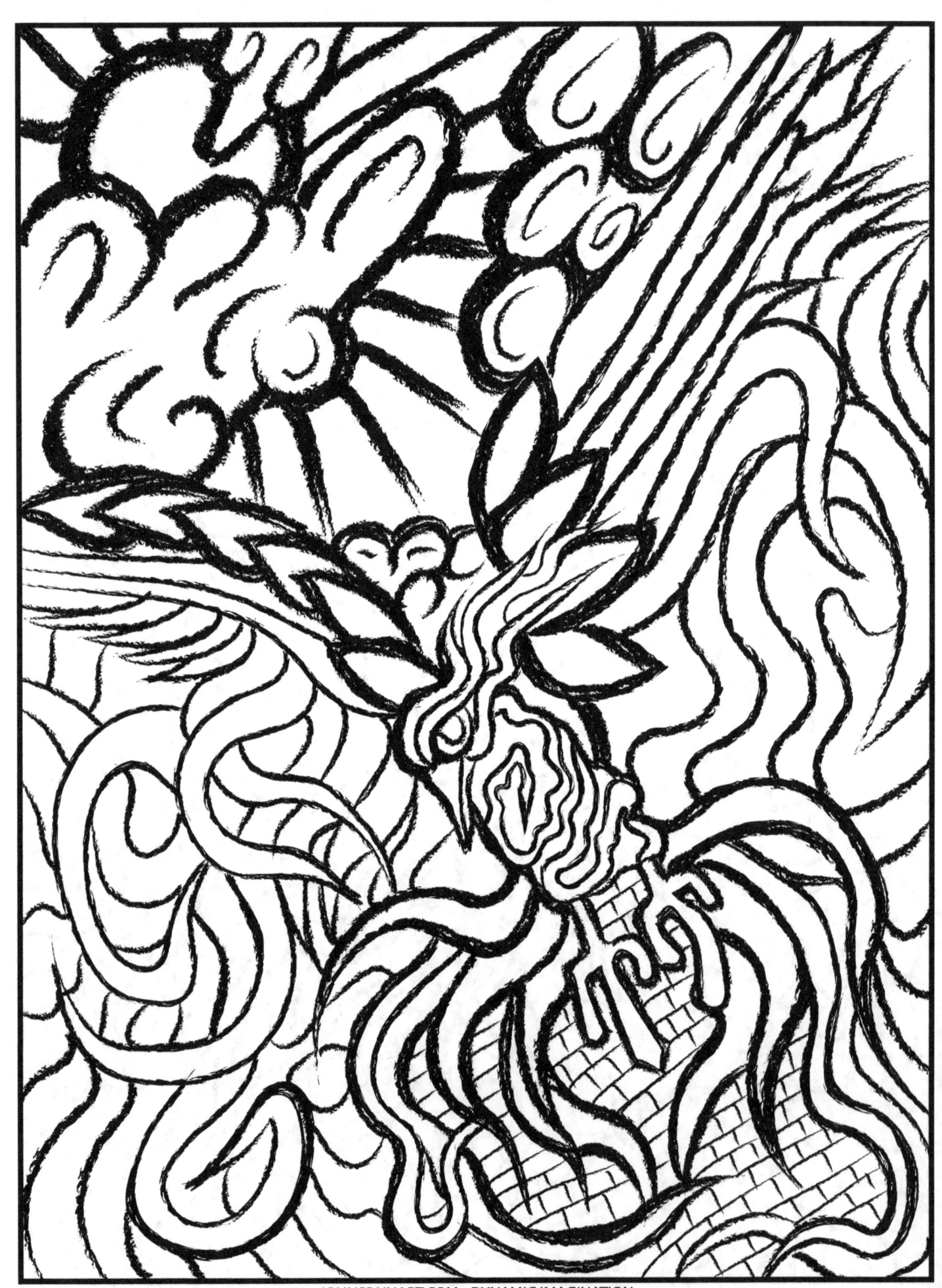
JOHNSPAINART.COM - DYNAMIC IMAGINATION

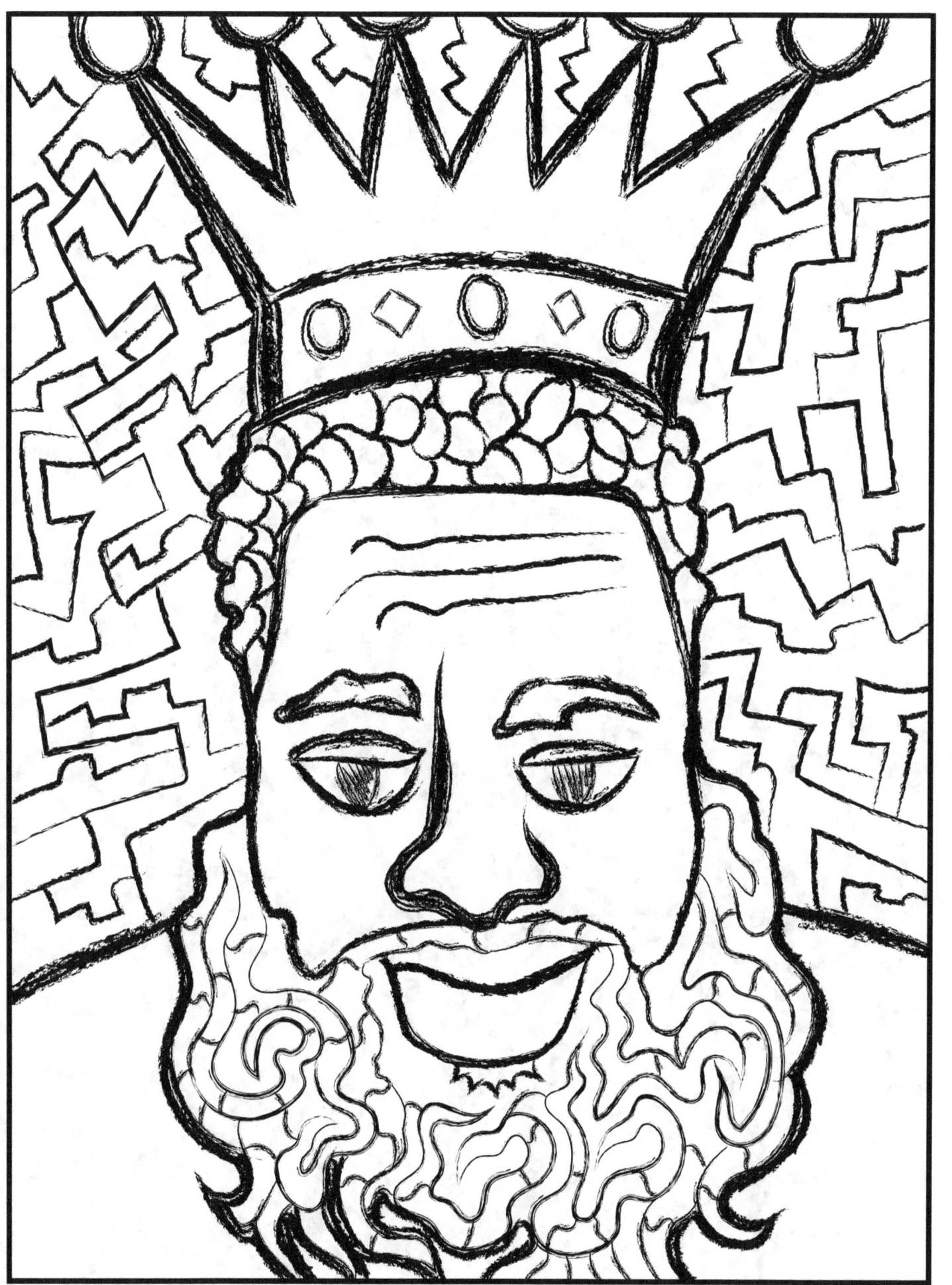

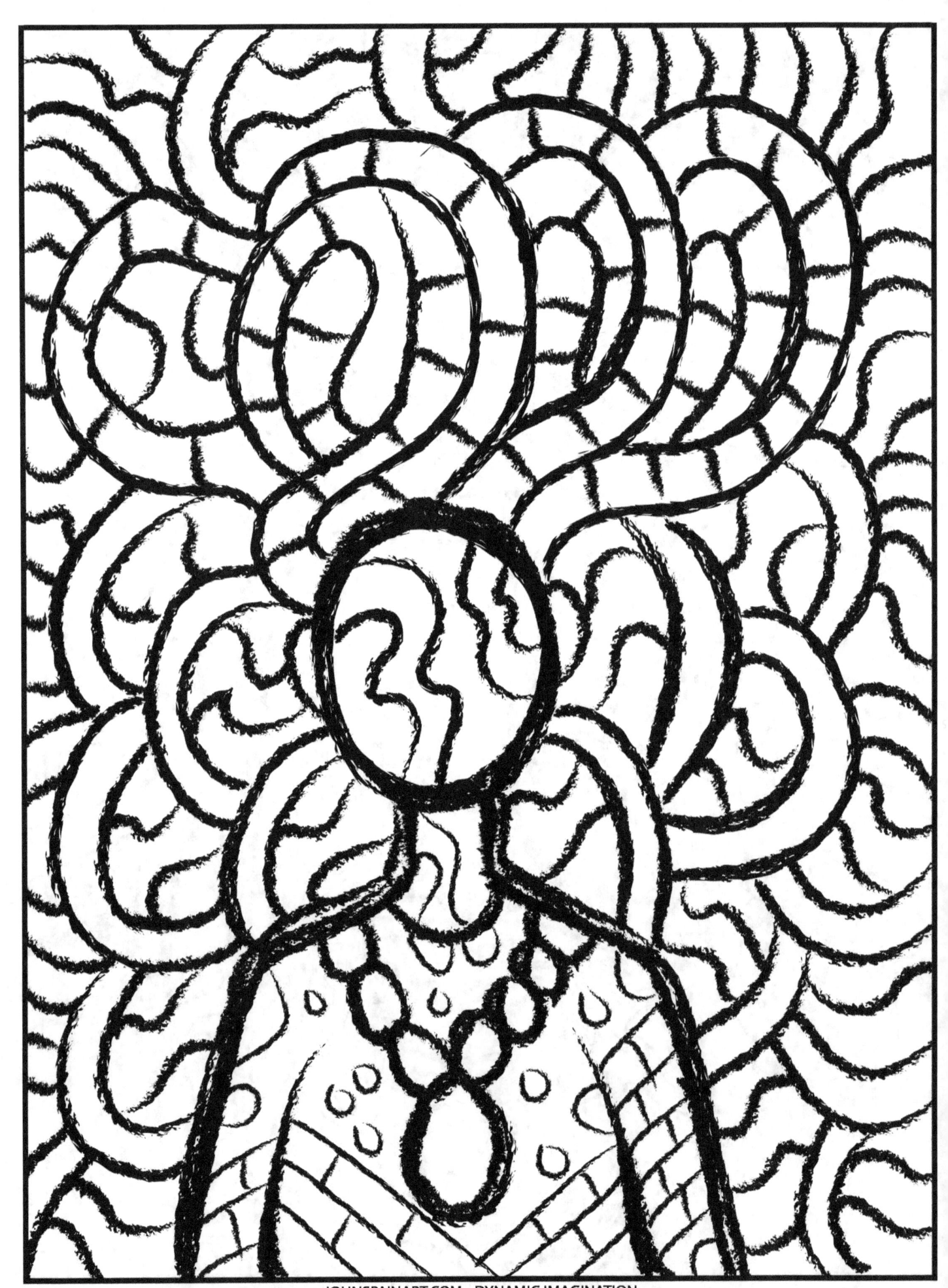

JOHNSPAINART.COM - DYNAMIC IMAGINATION

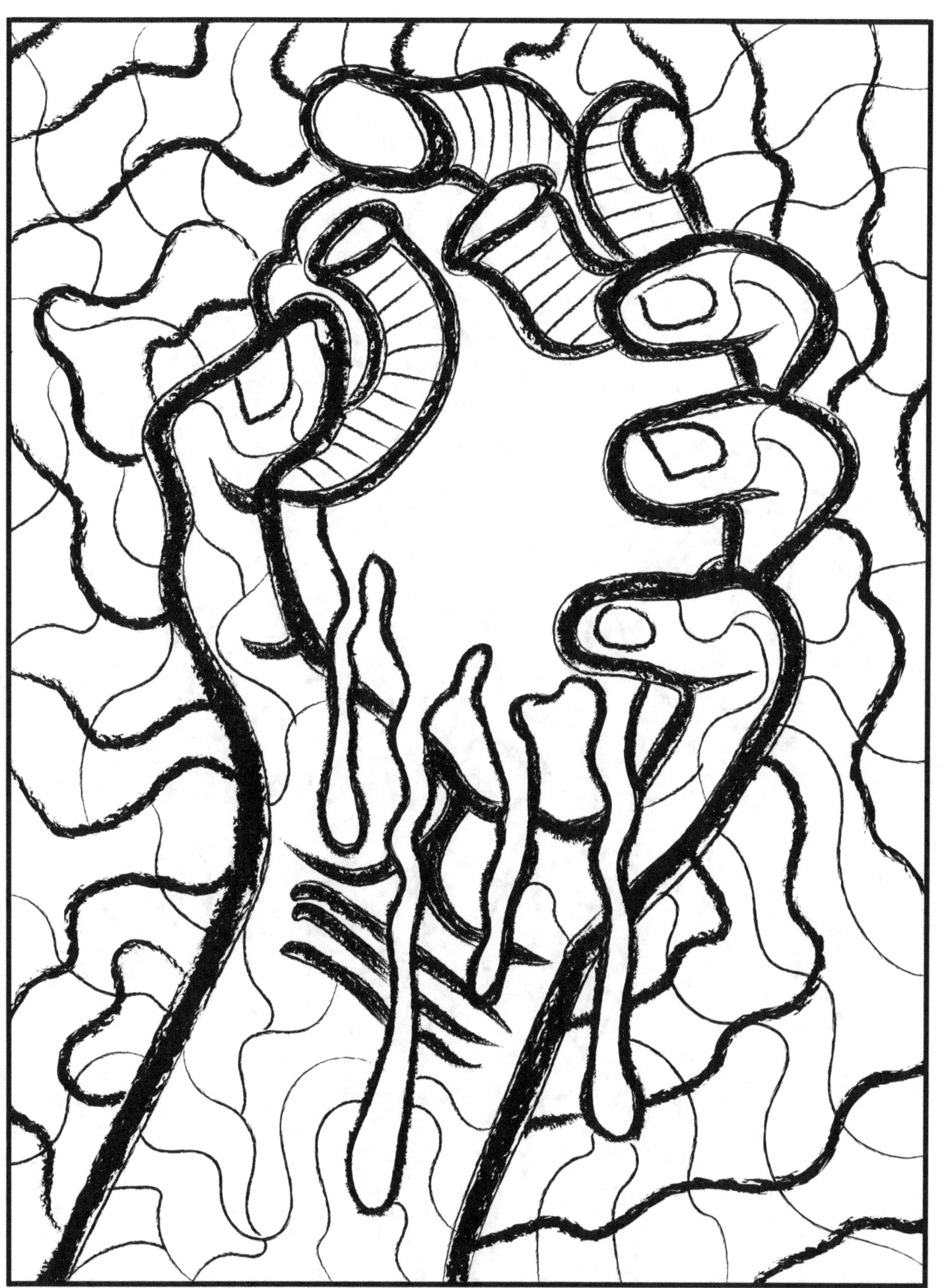

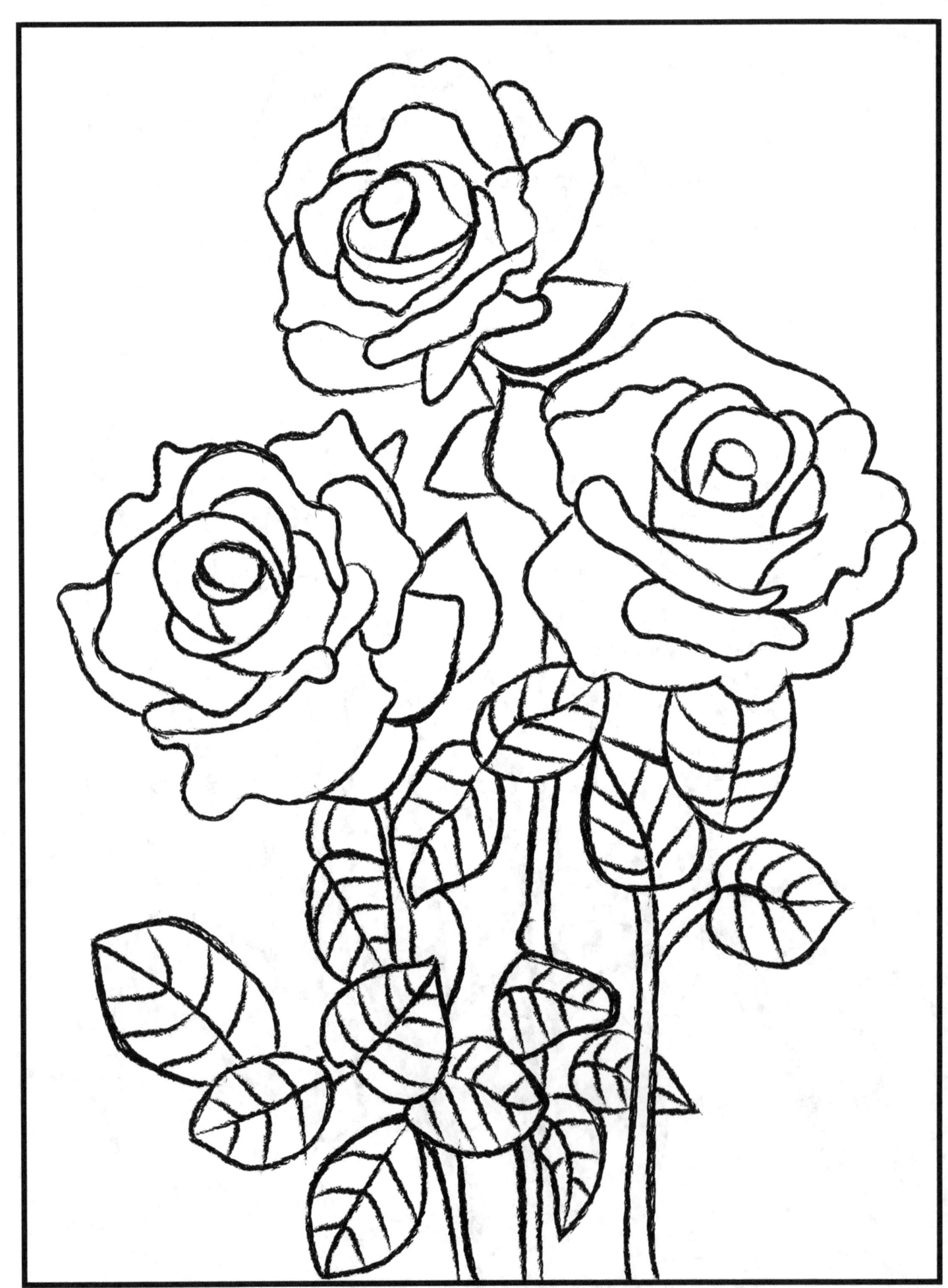

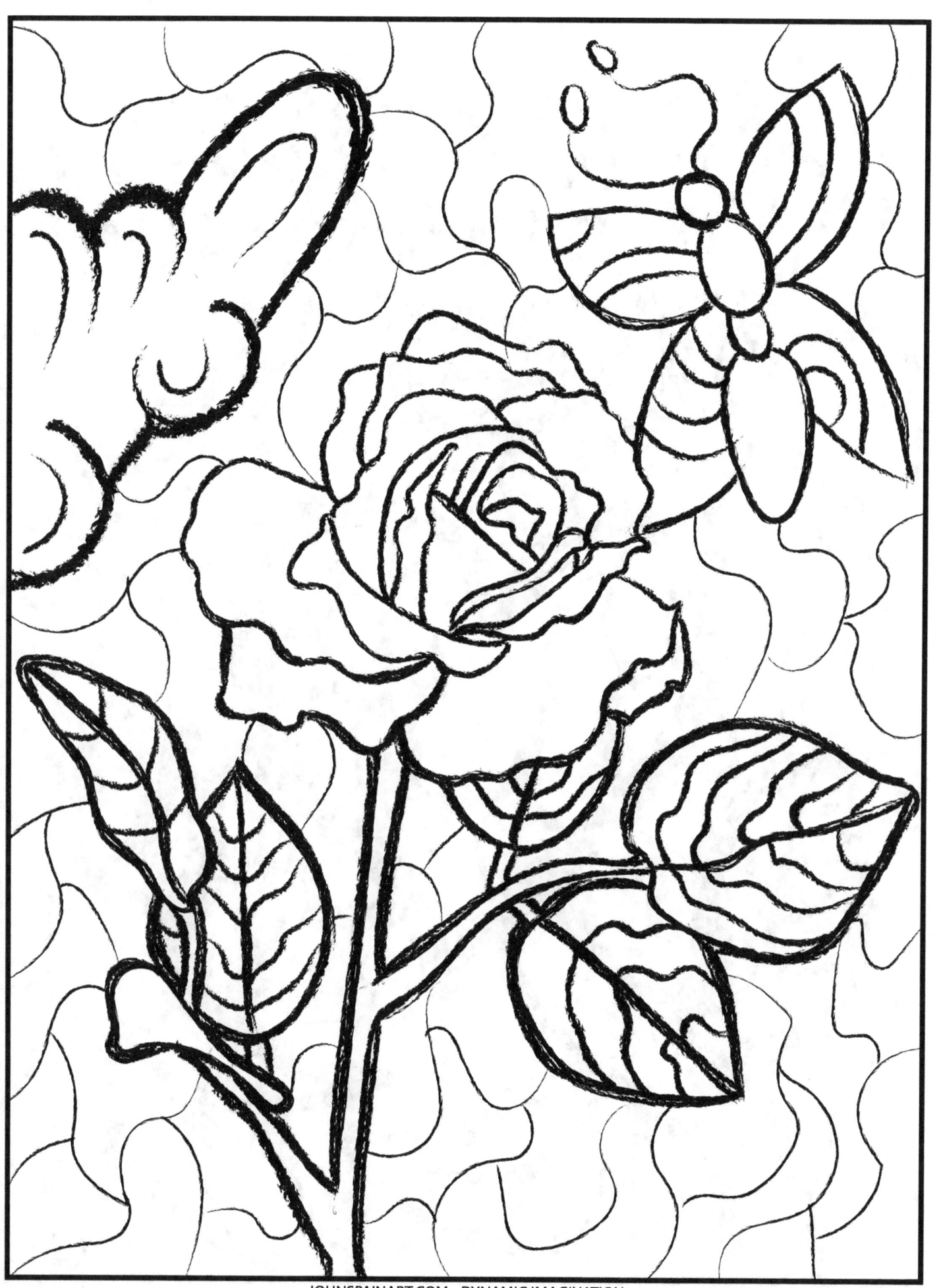

JOHNSPAINART.COM - DYNAMIC IMAGINATION

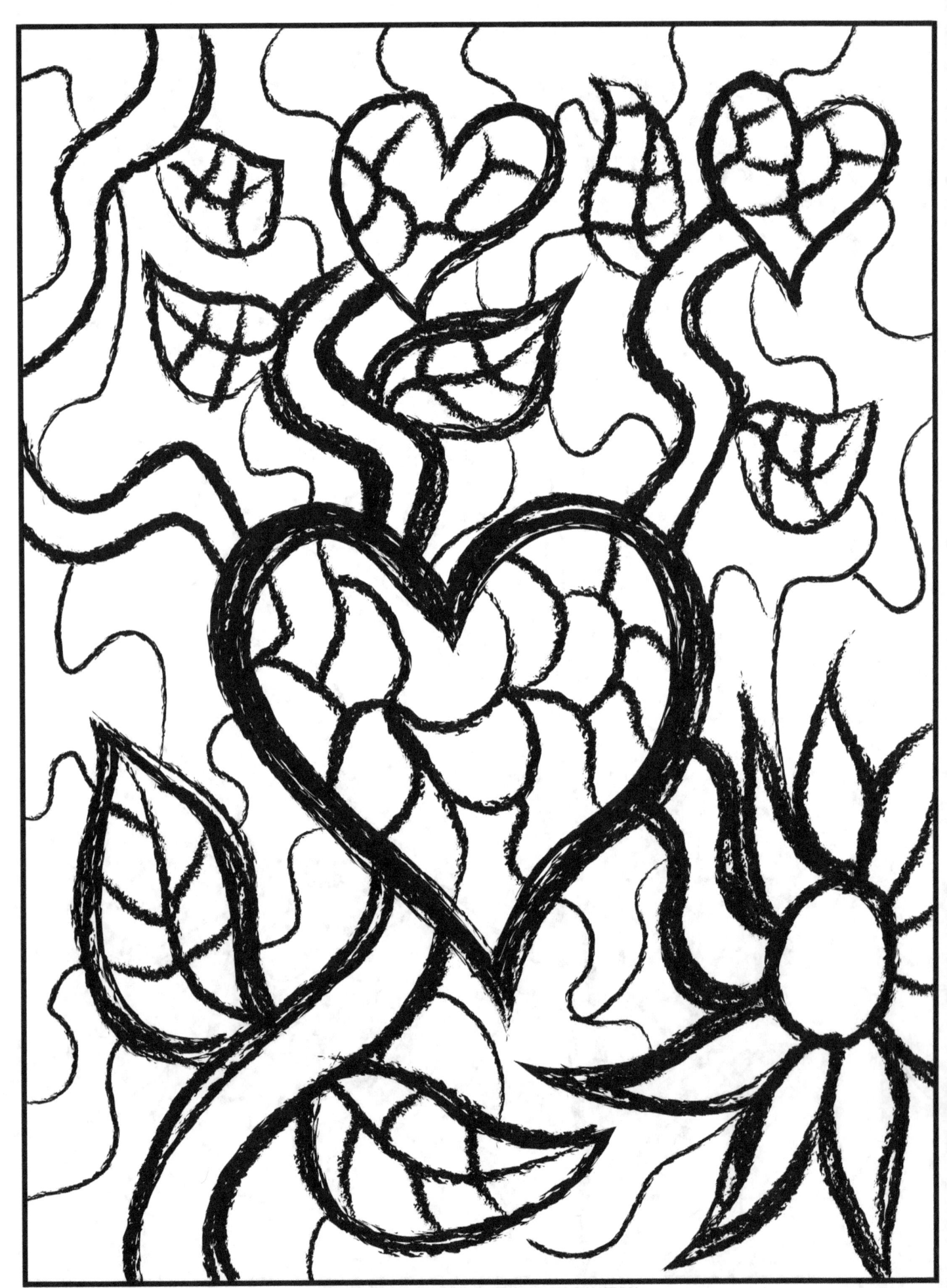

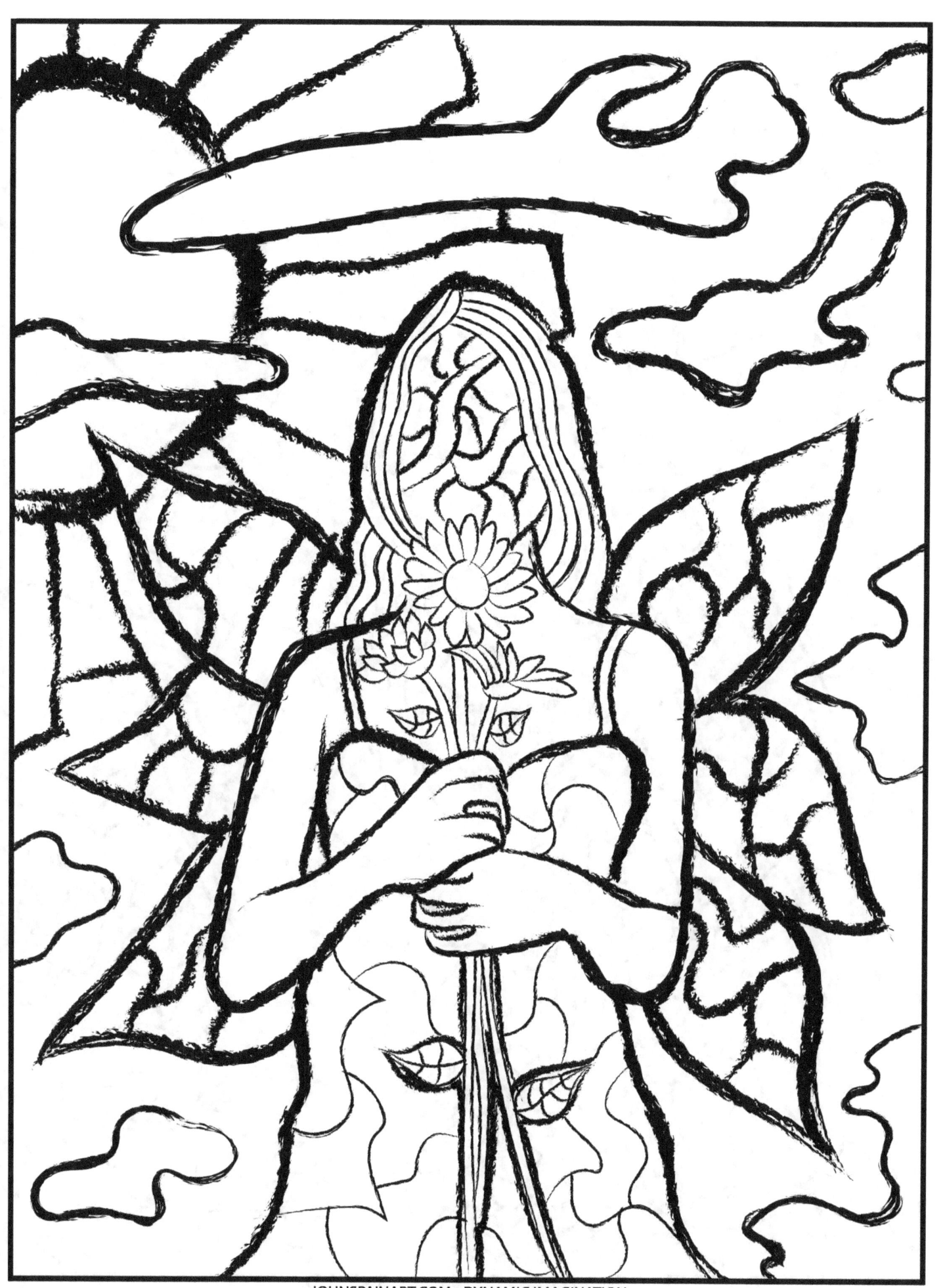

JOHNSPAINART.COM - DYNAMIC IMAGINATION

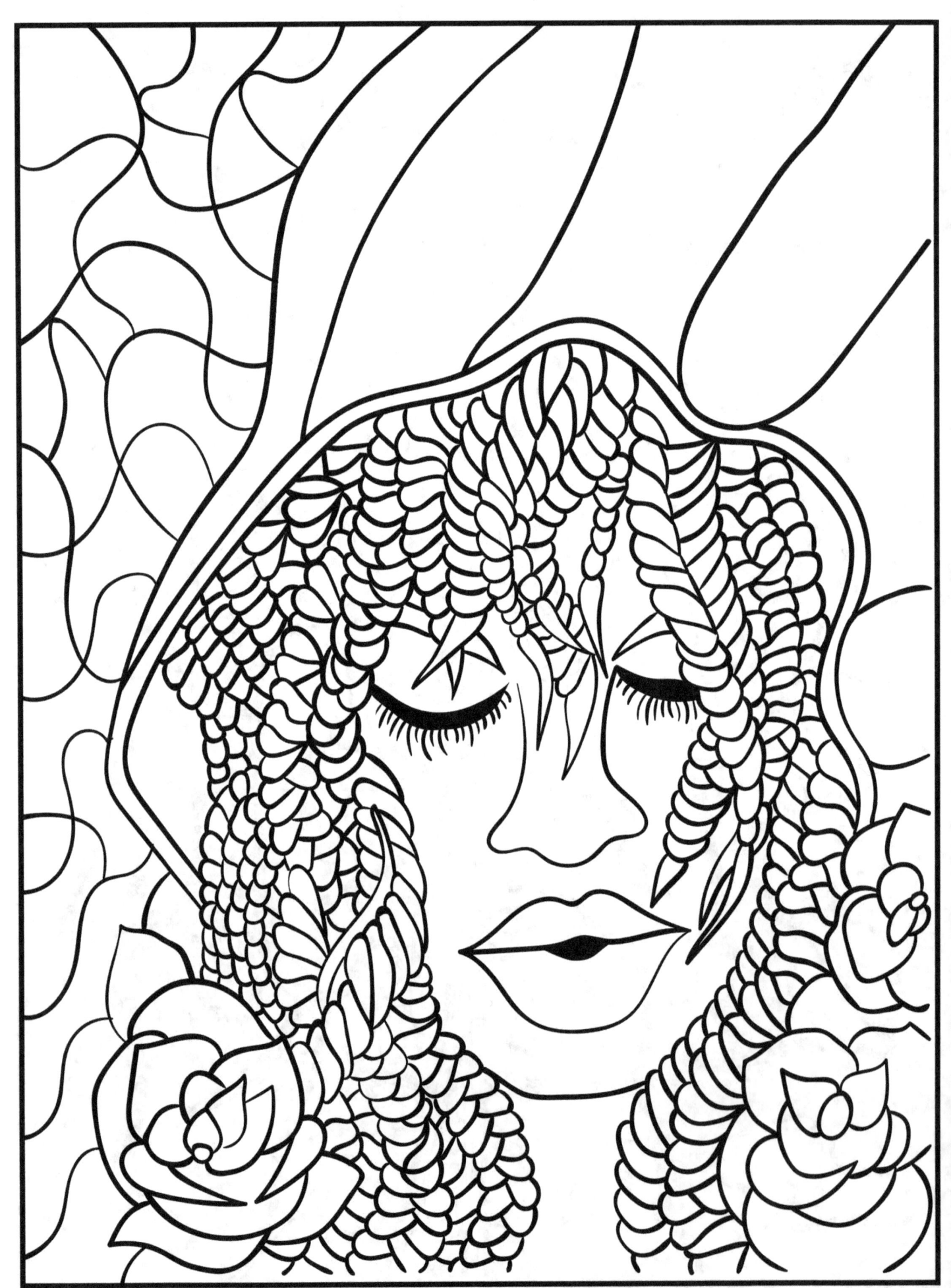

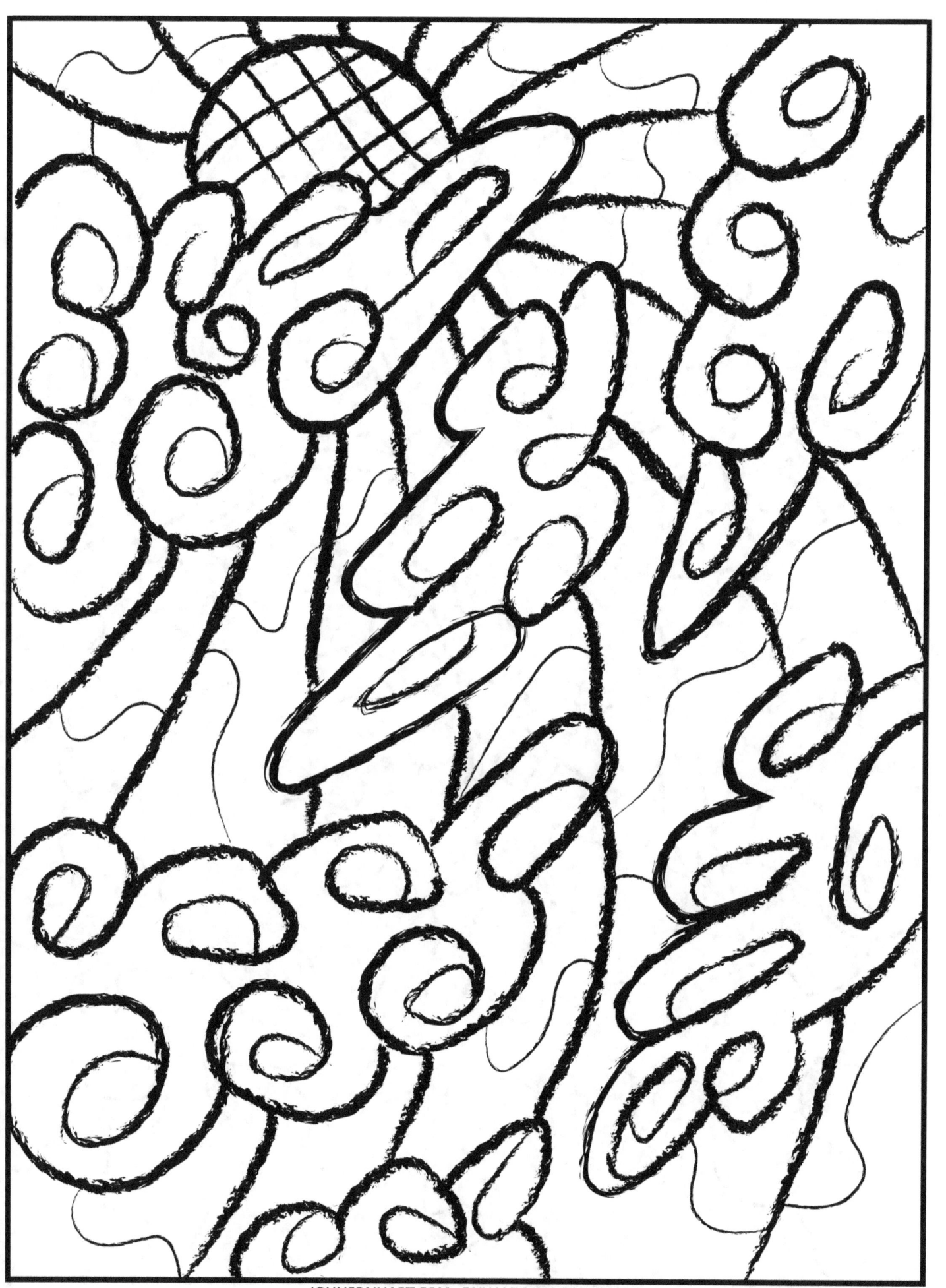

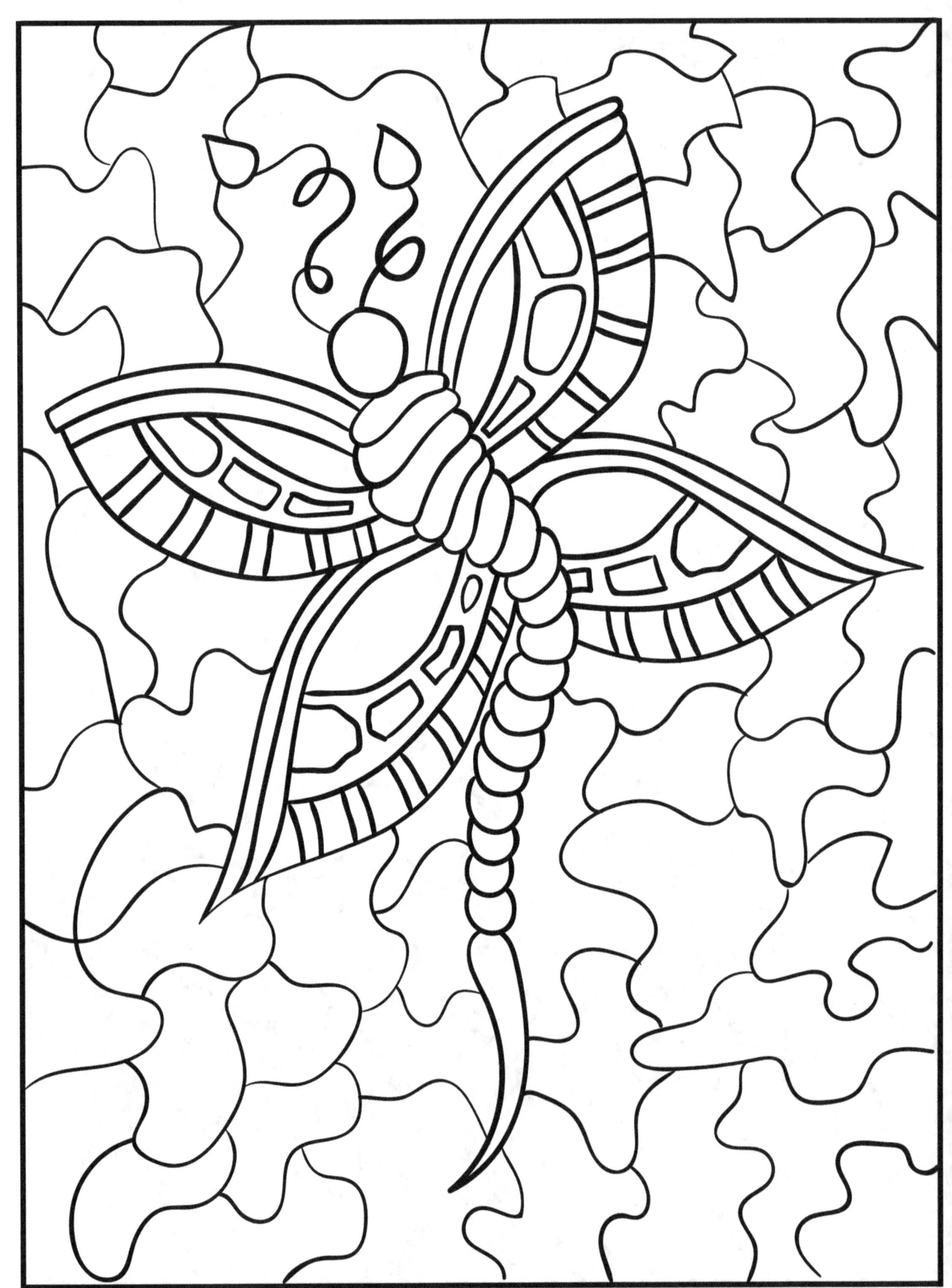

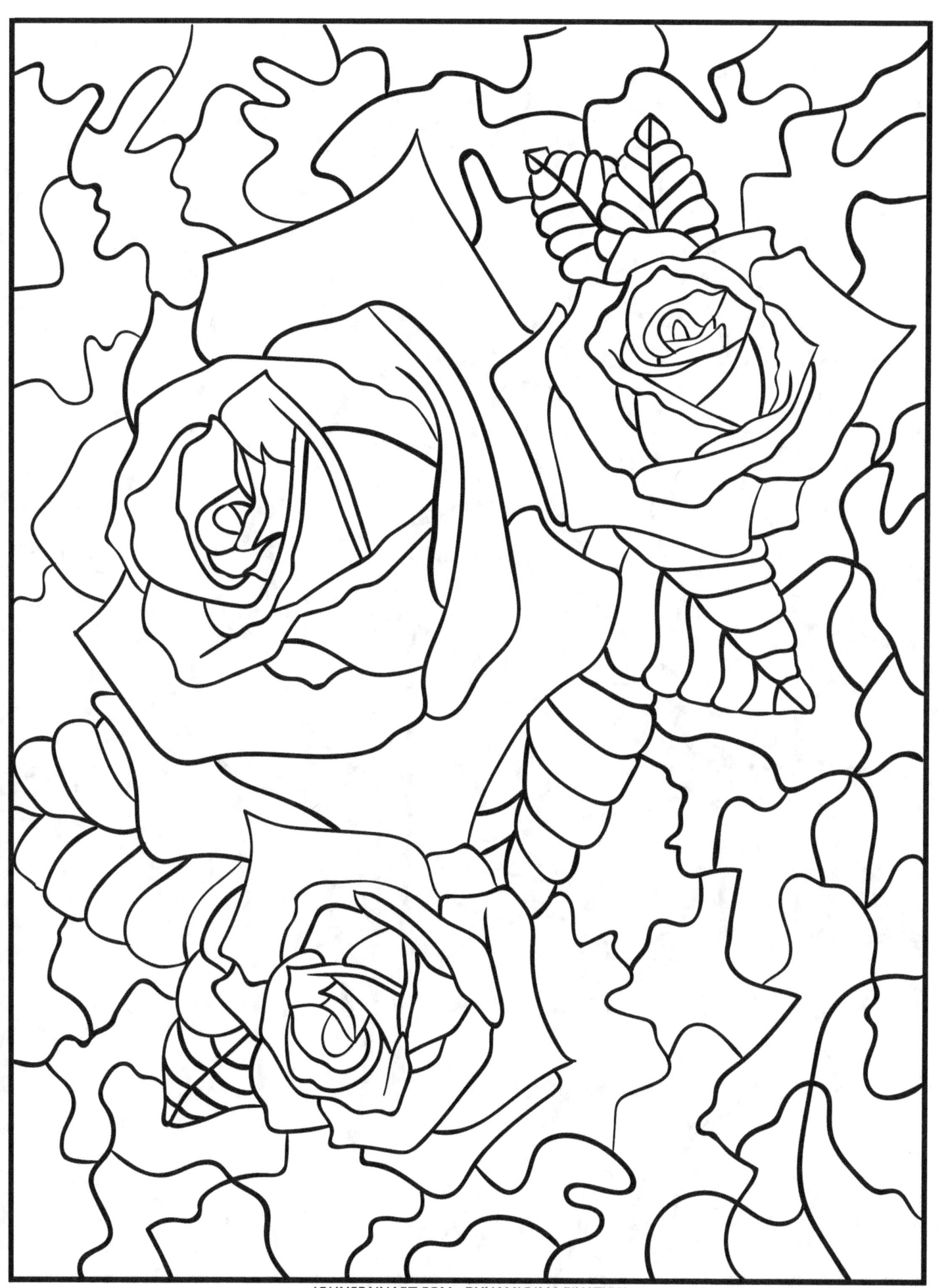

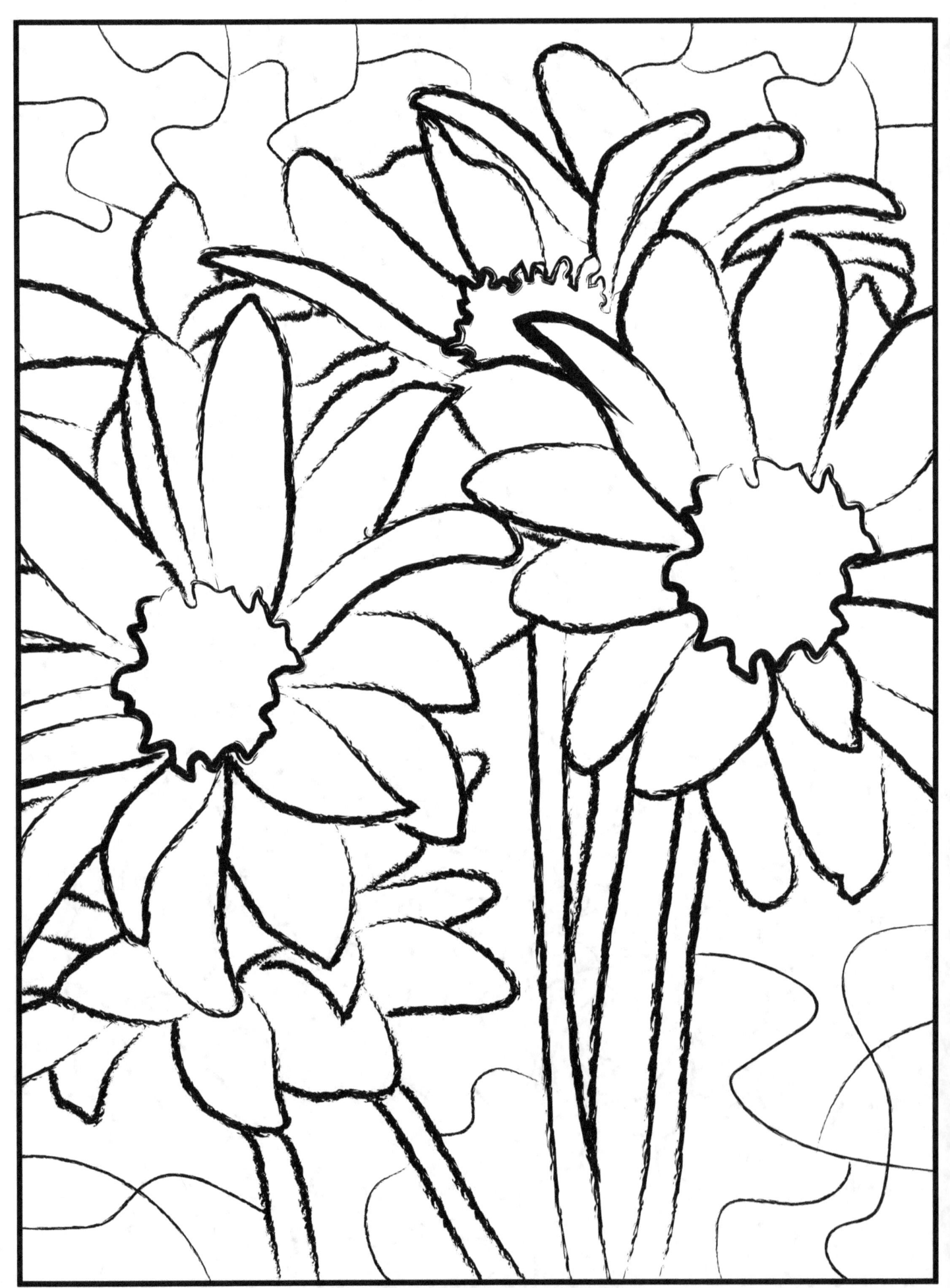
JOHNSPAINART.COM - DYNAMIC IMAGINATION

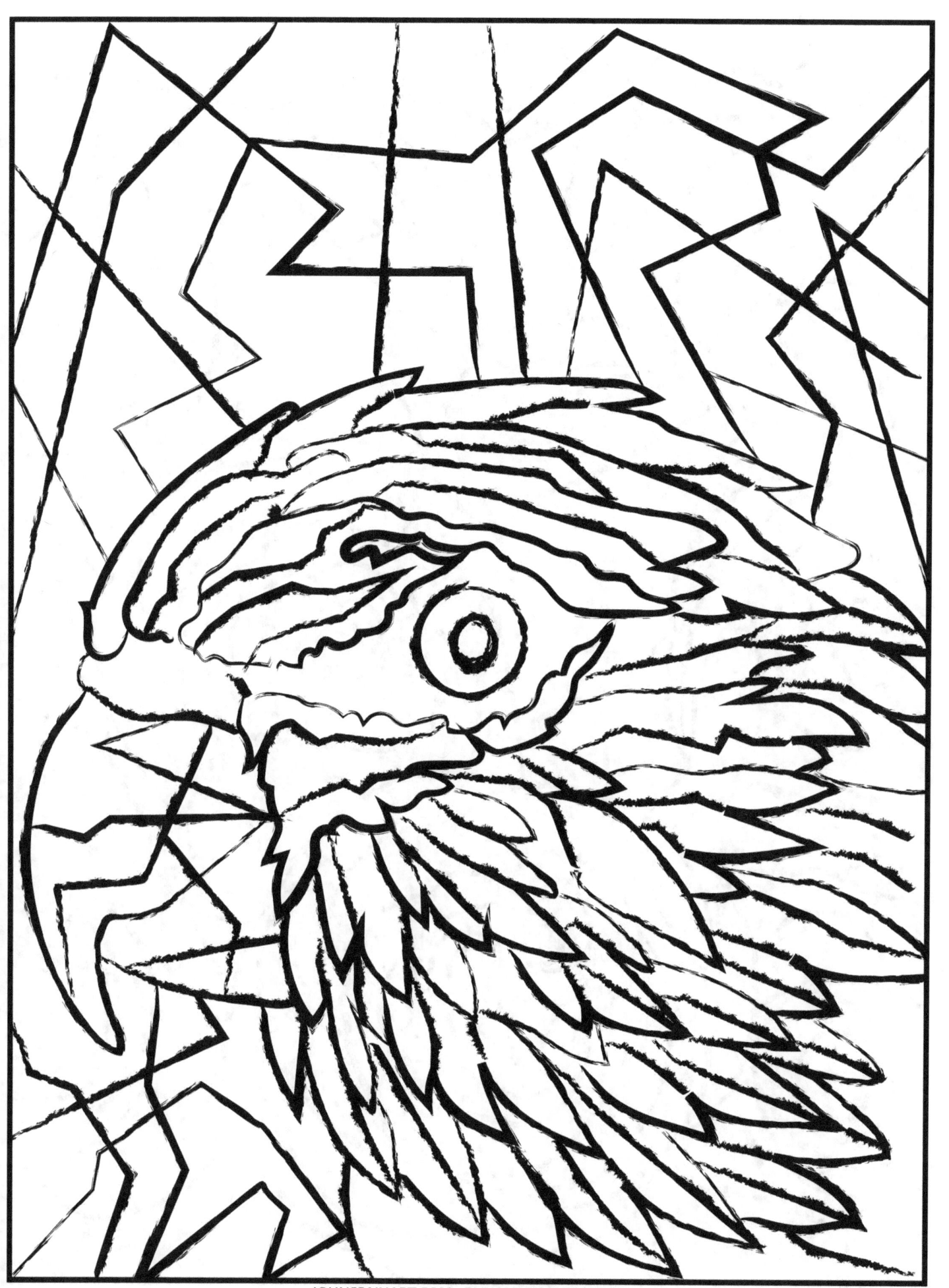

JOHNSPAINART.COM - DYNAMIC IMAGINATION

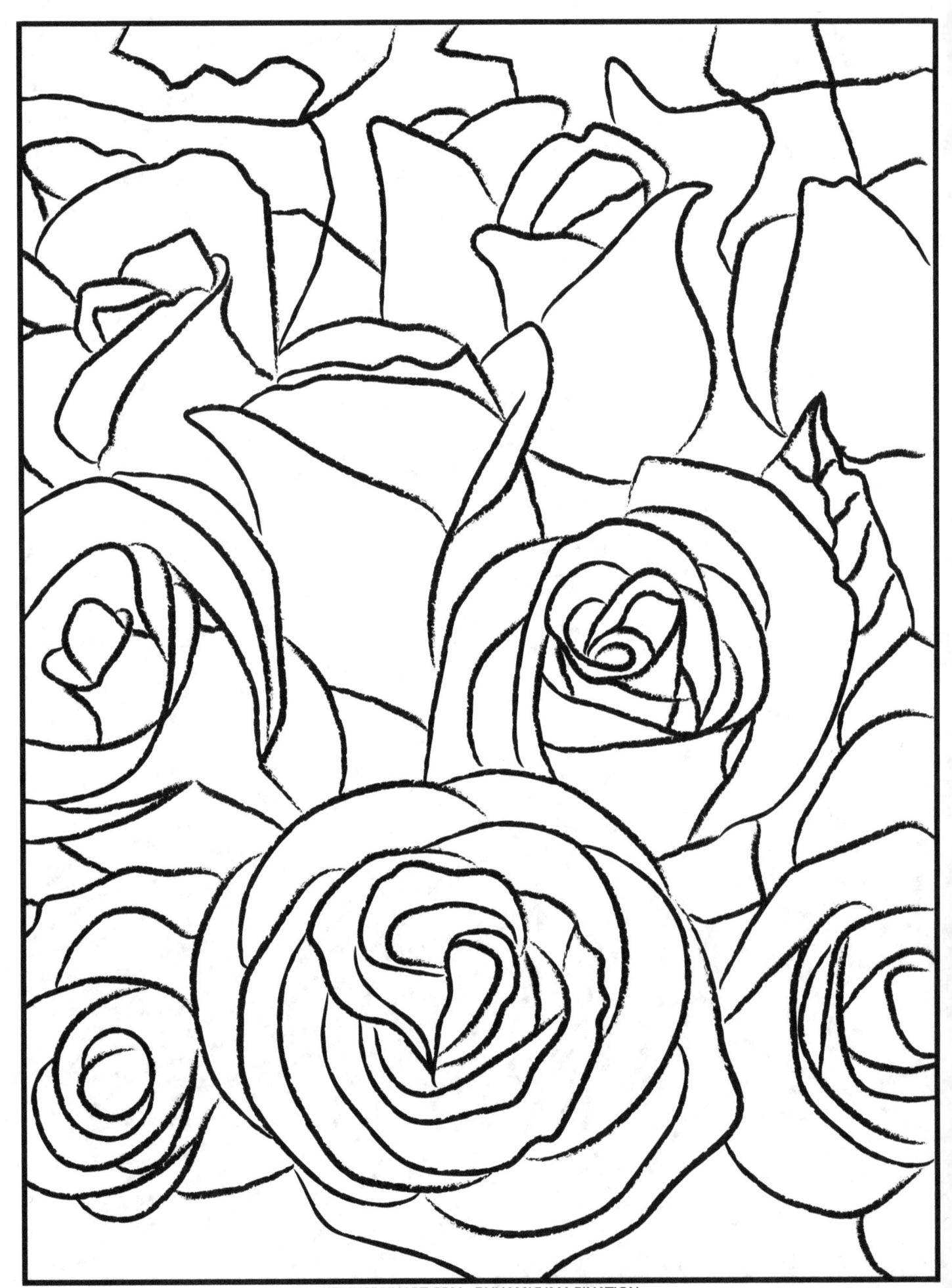

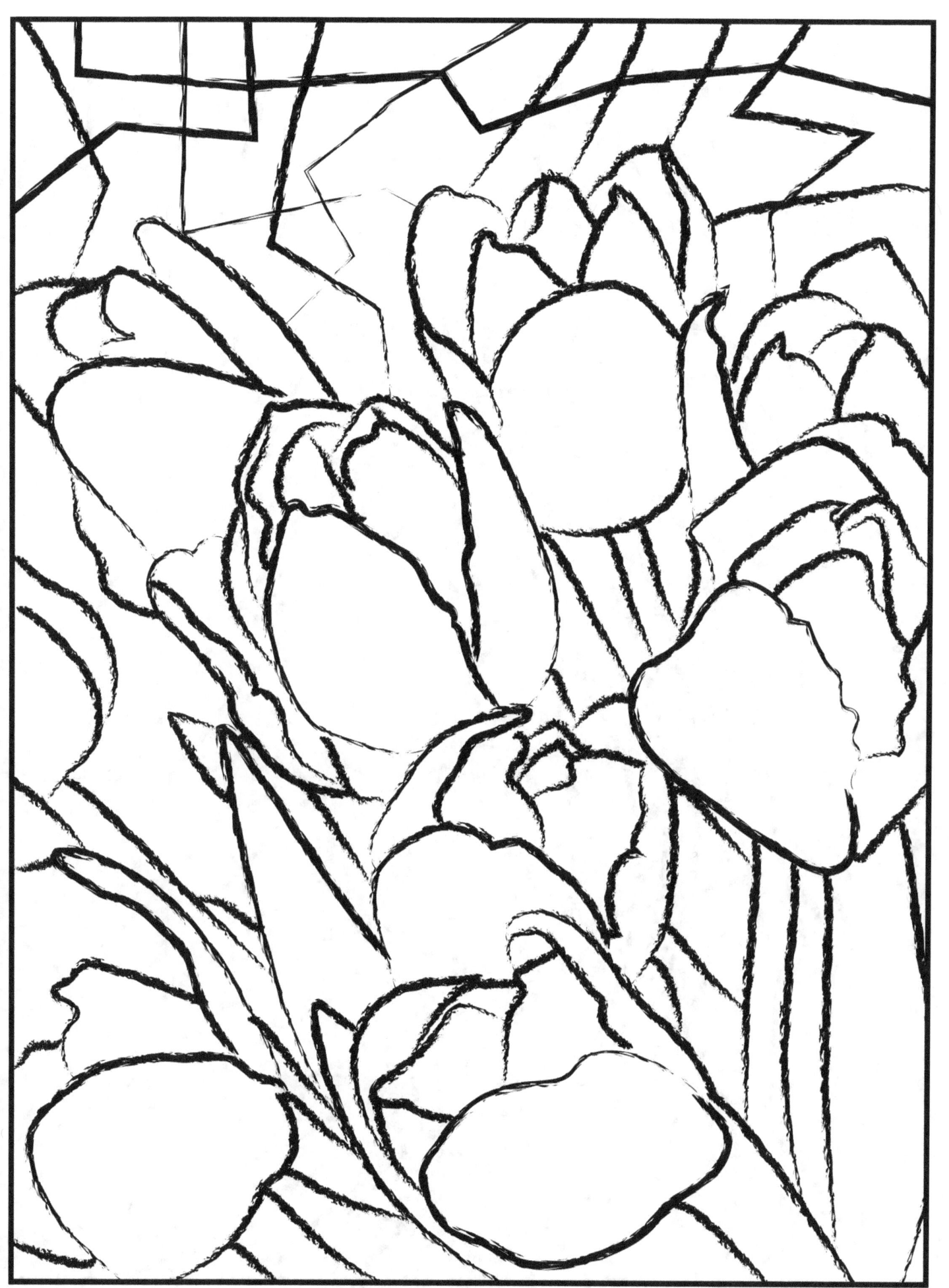

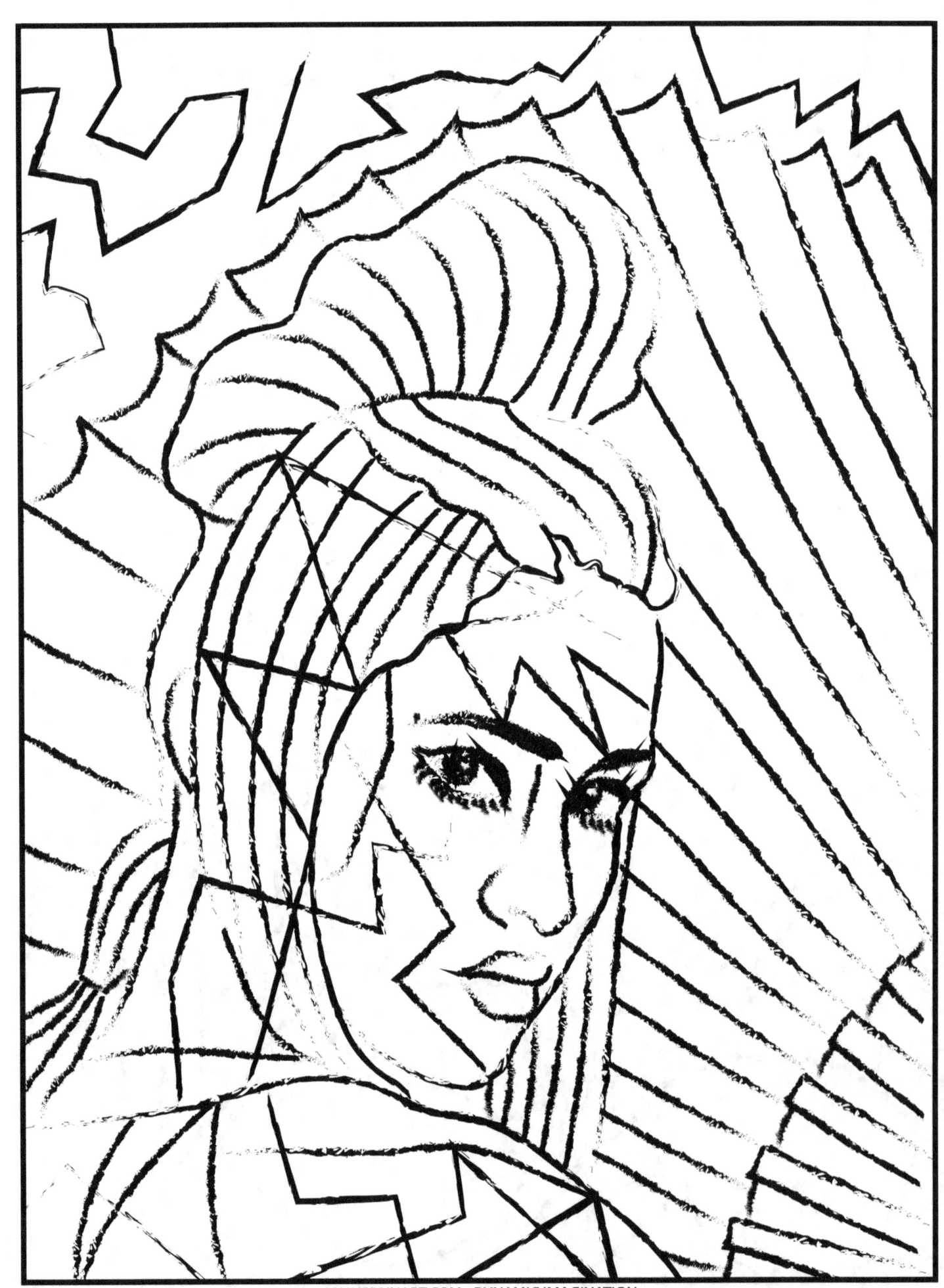

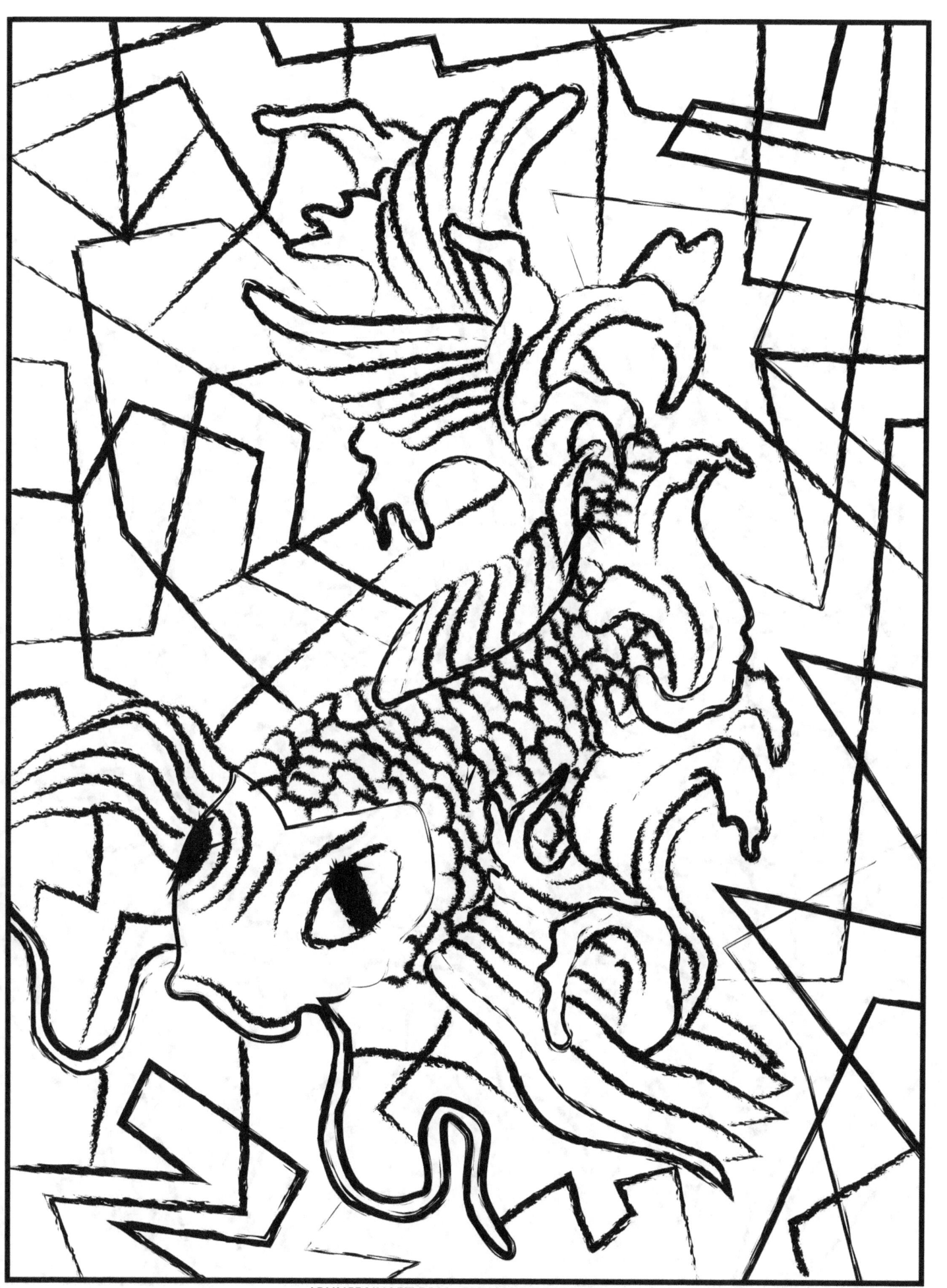

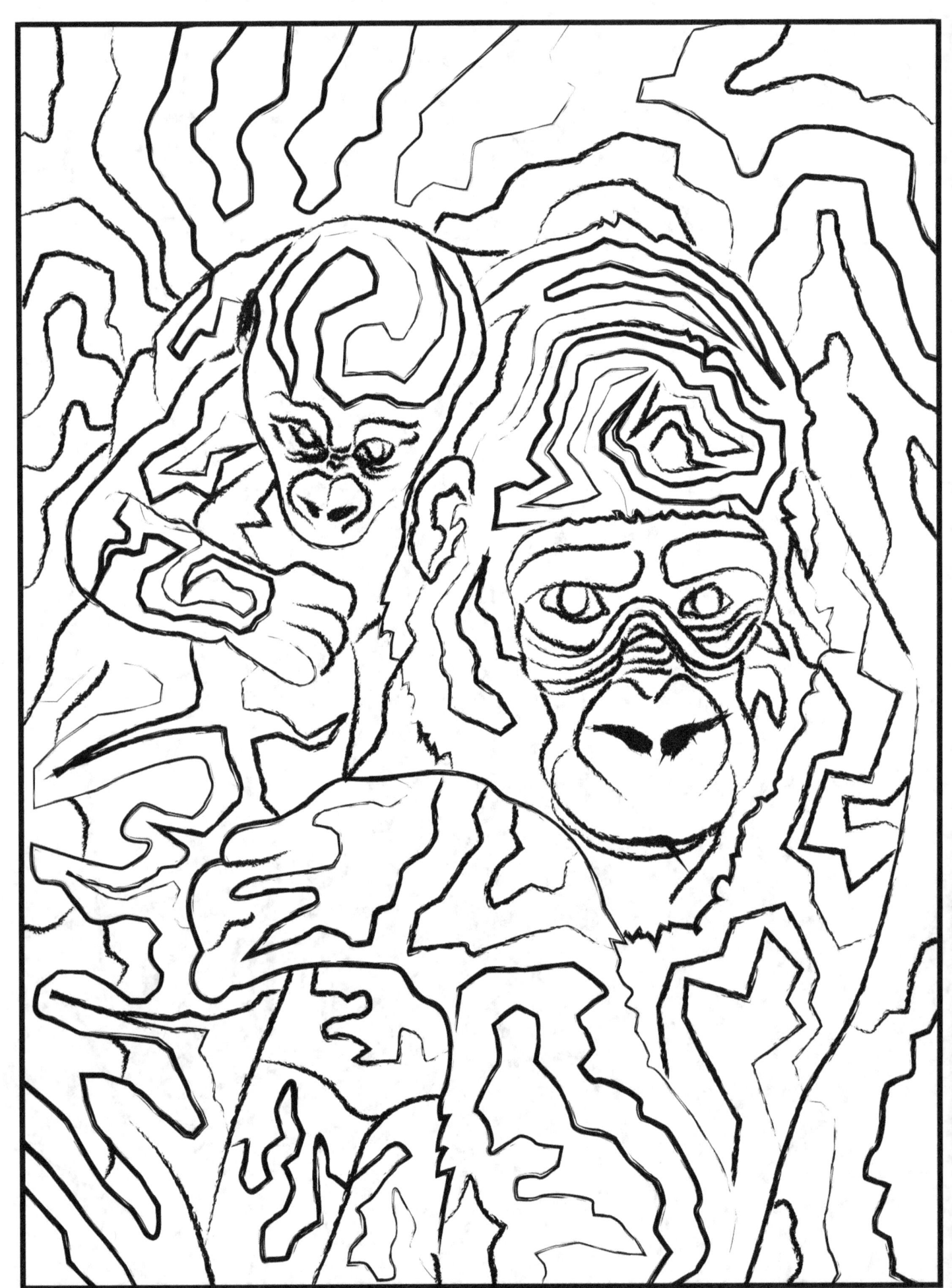
JOHNSPAINART.COM - DYNAMIC IMAGINATION

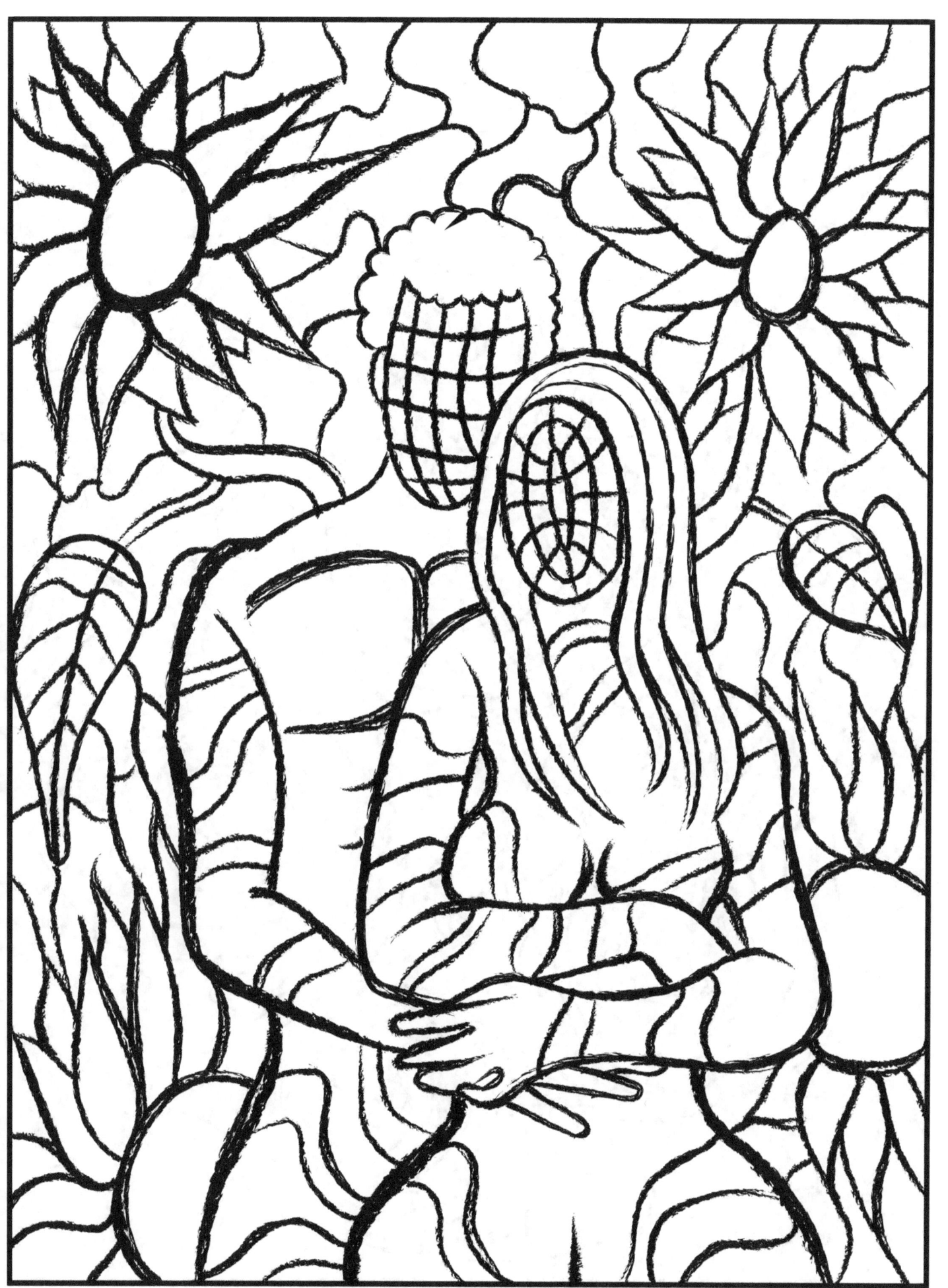

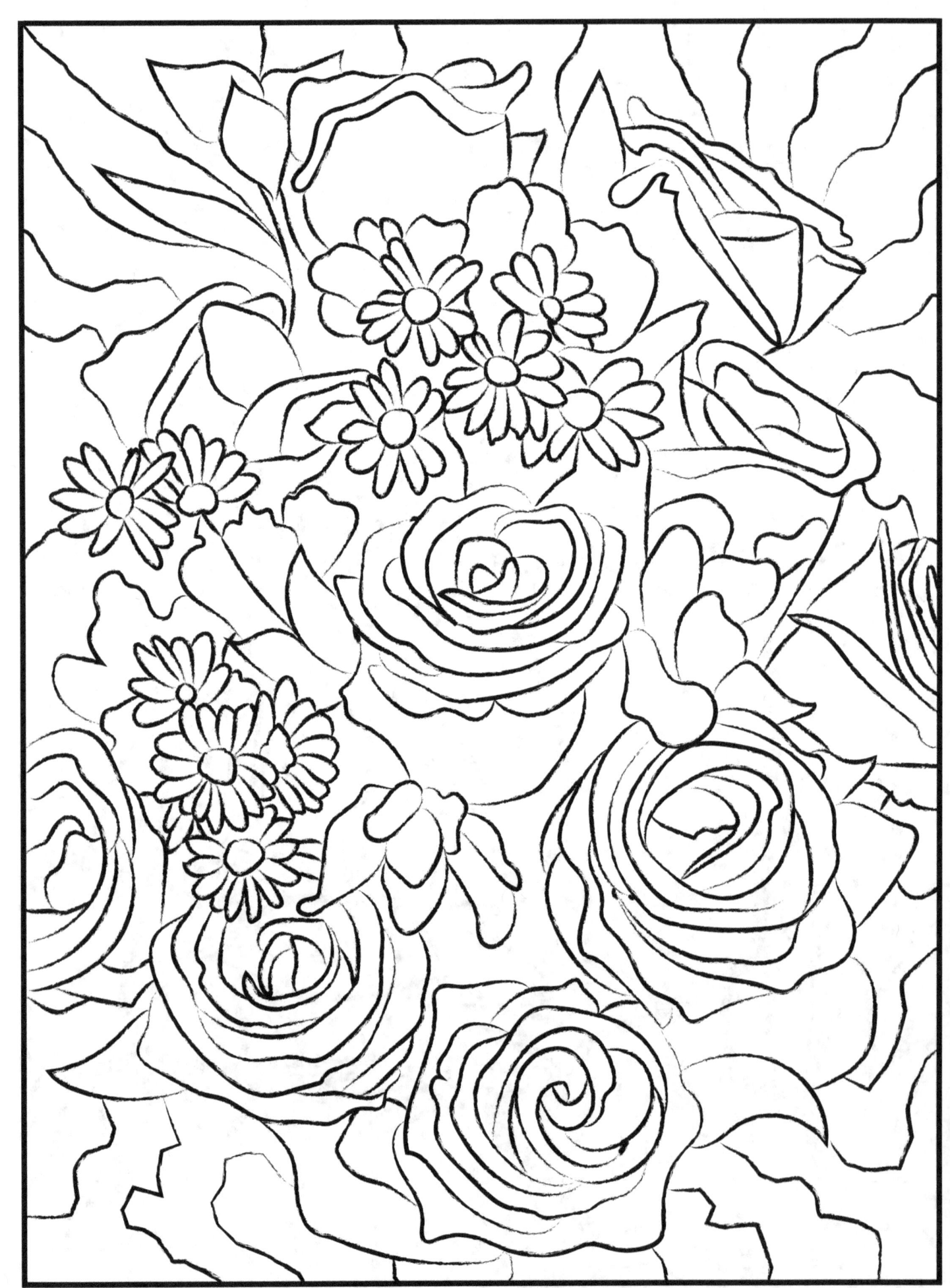

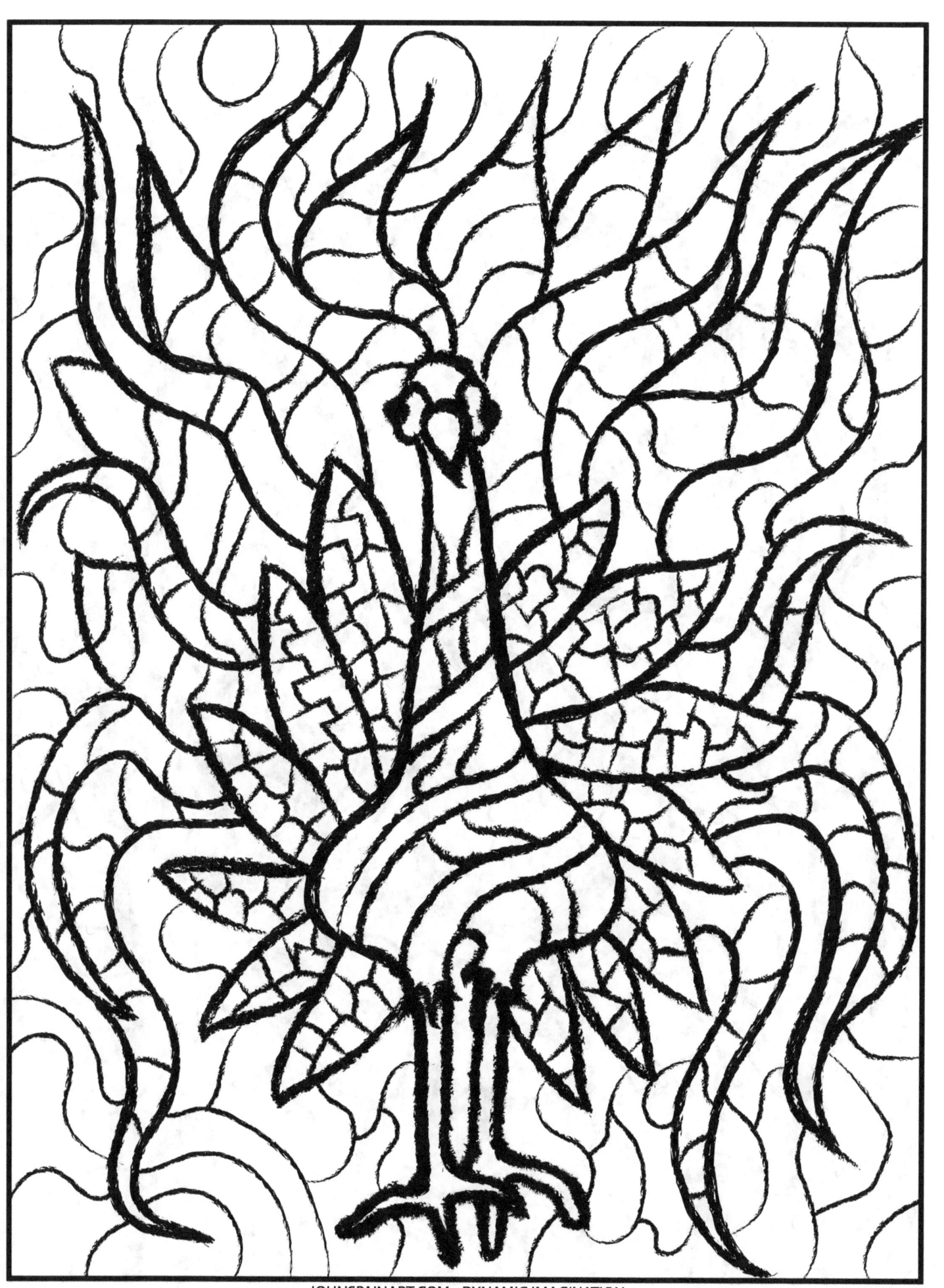

JOHNSPAINART.COM - DYNAMIC IMAGINATION

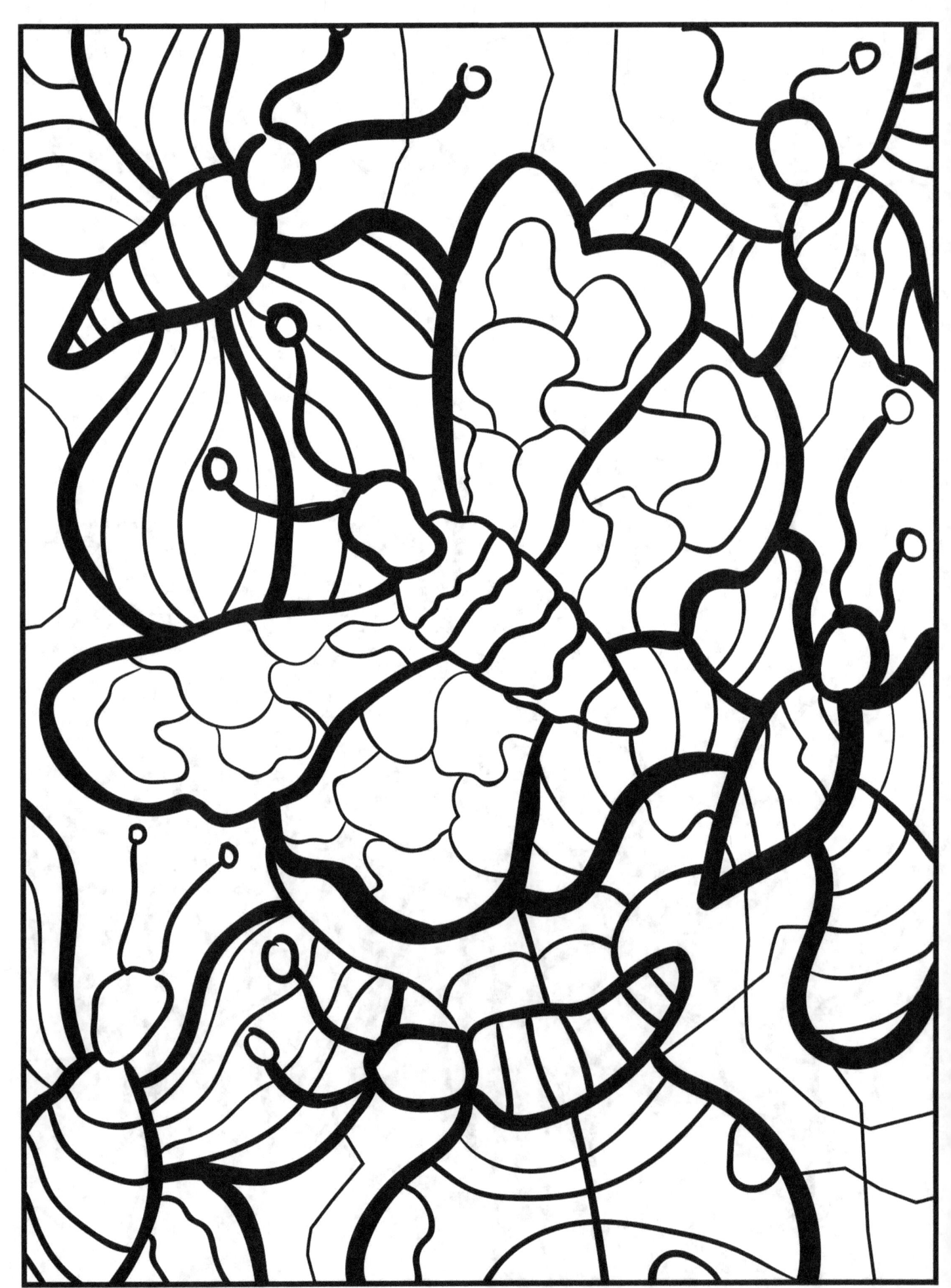
JOHNSPAINART.COM - DYNAMIC IMAGINATION

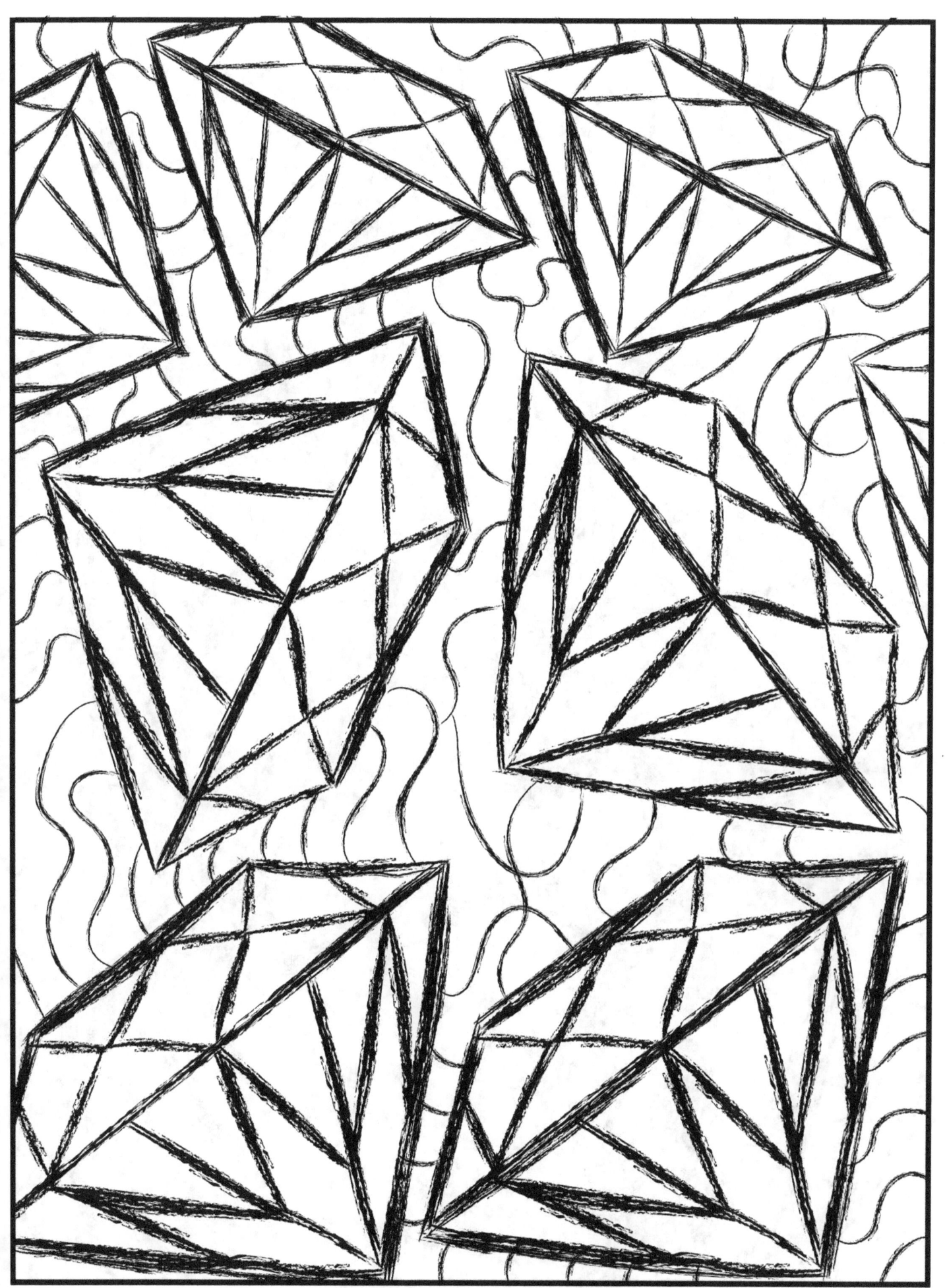
JOHNSPAINART.COM - DYNAMIC IMAGINATION

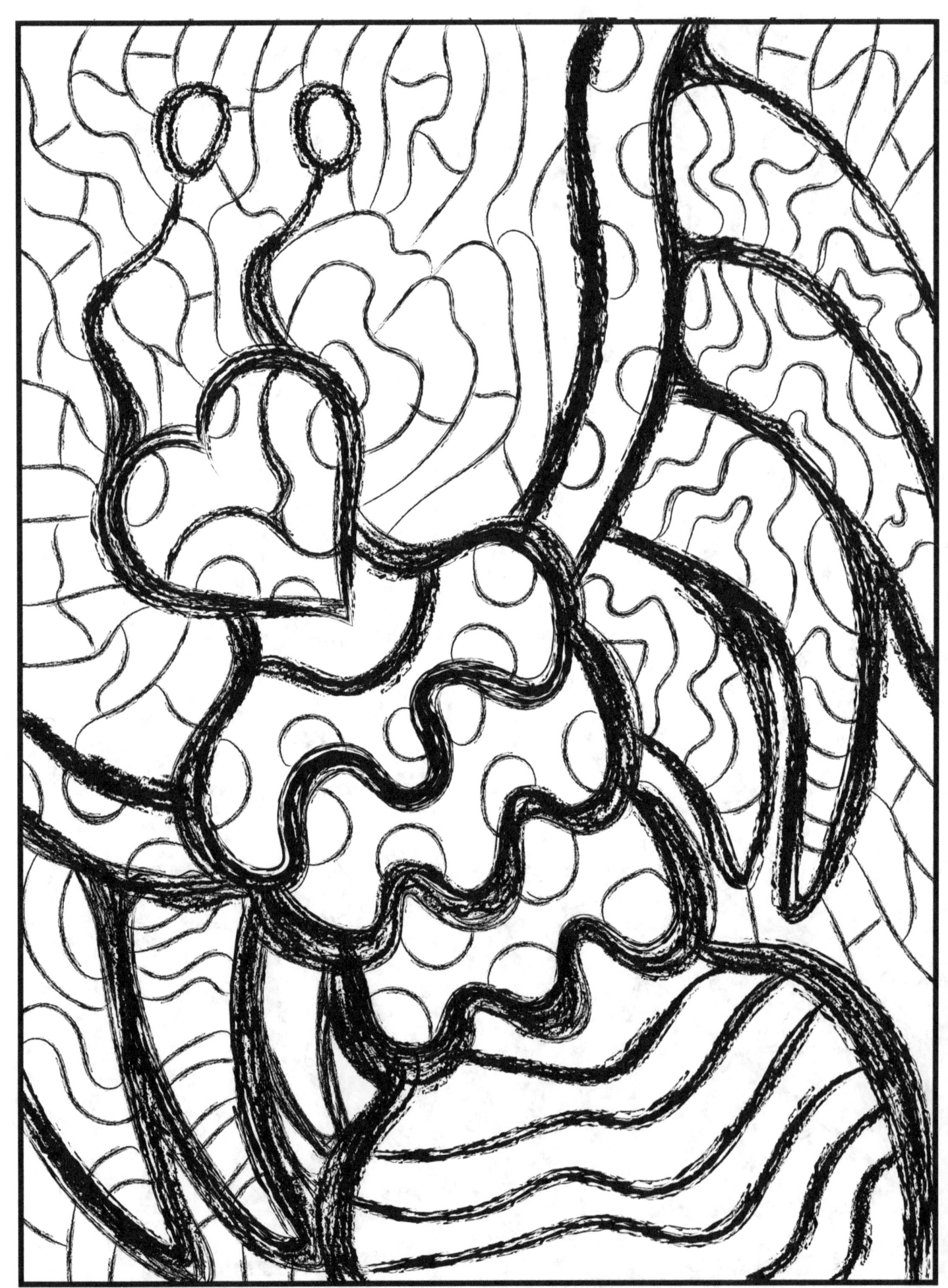

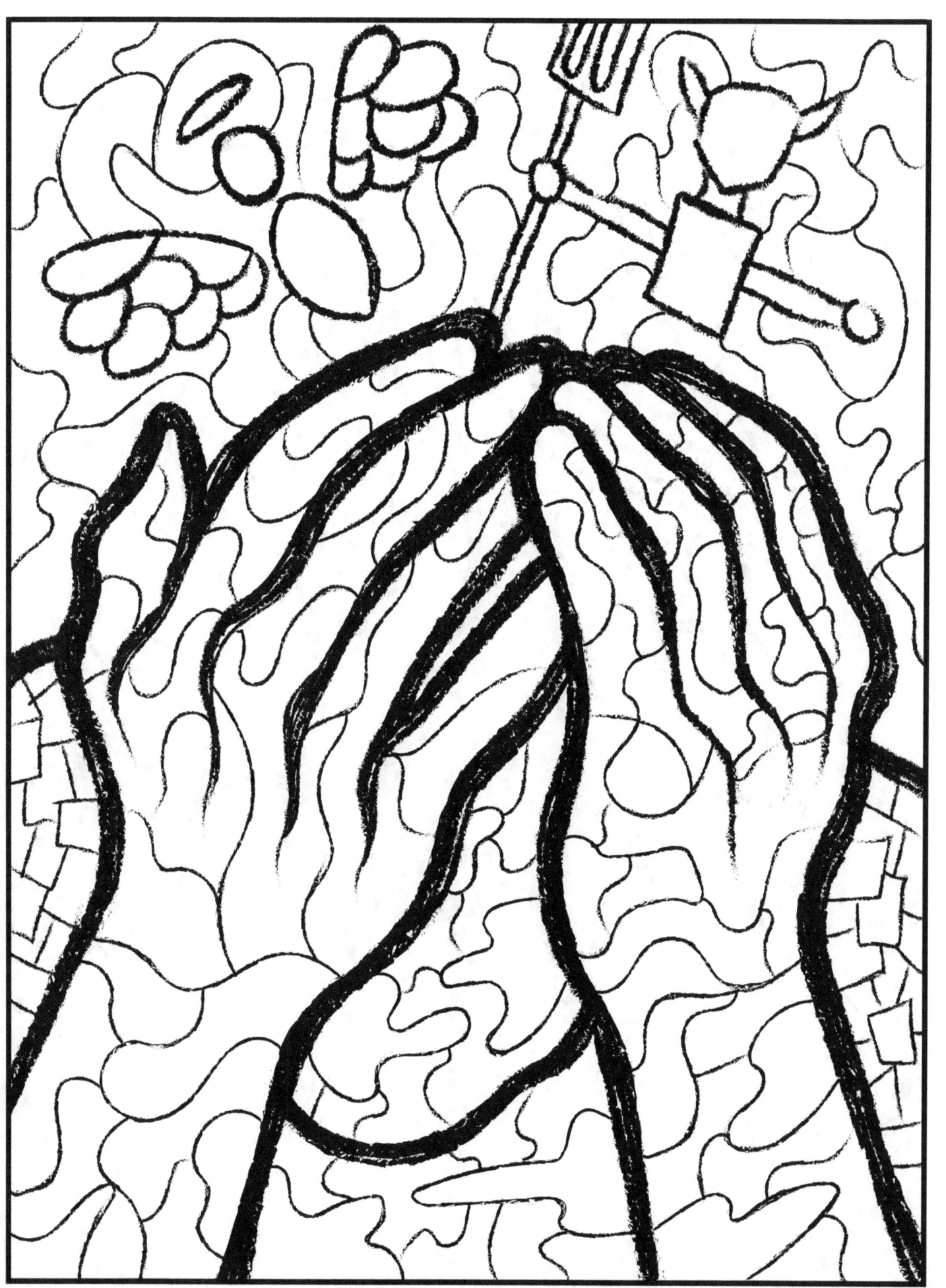

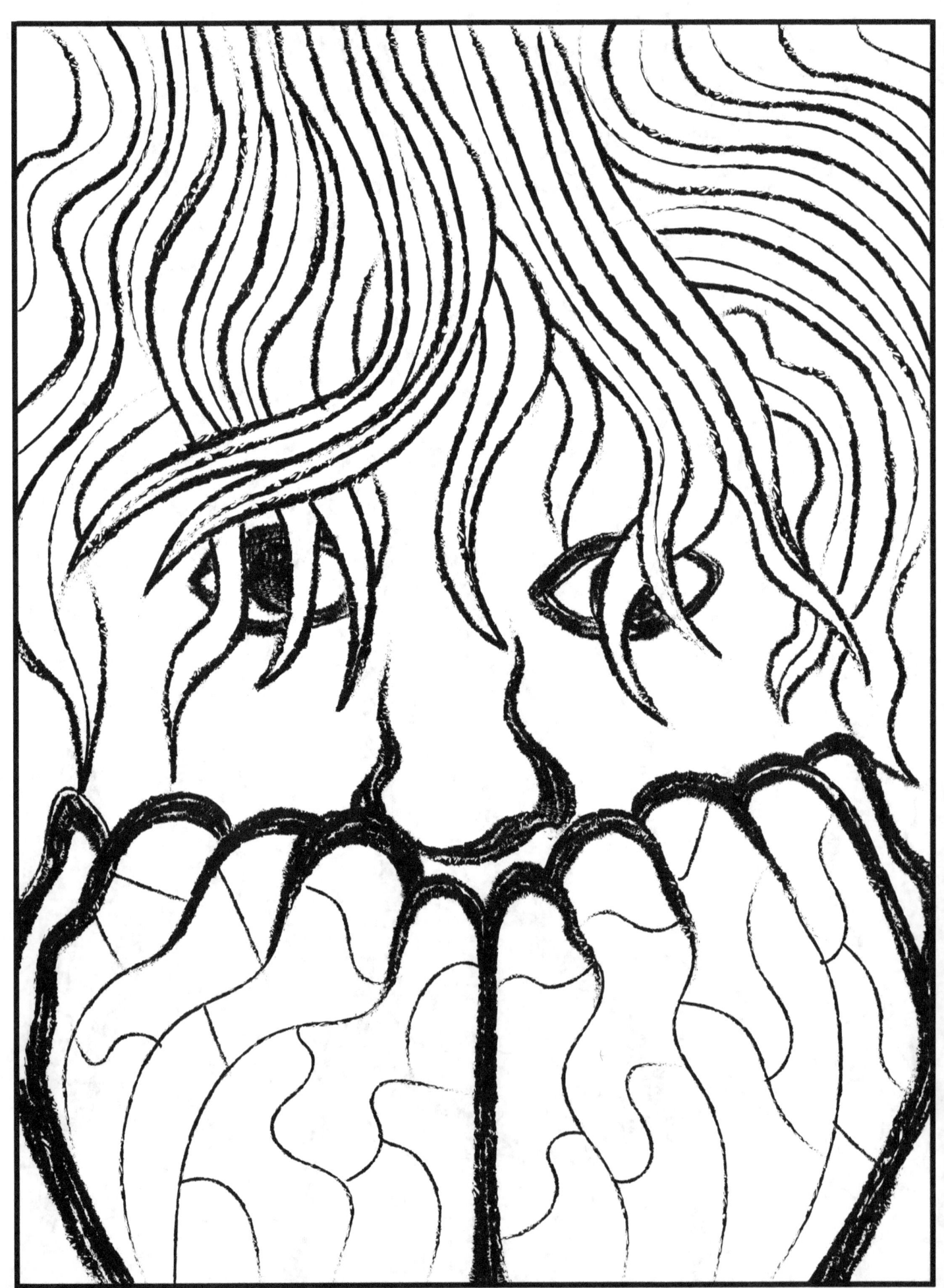

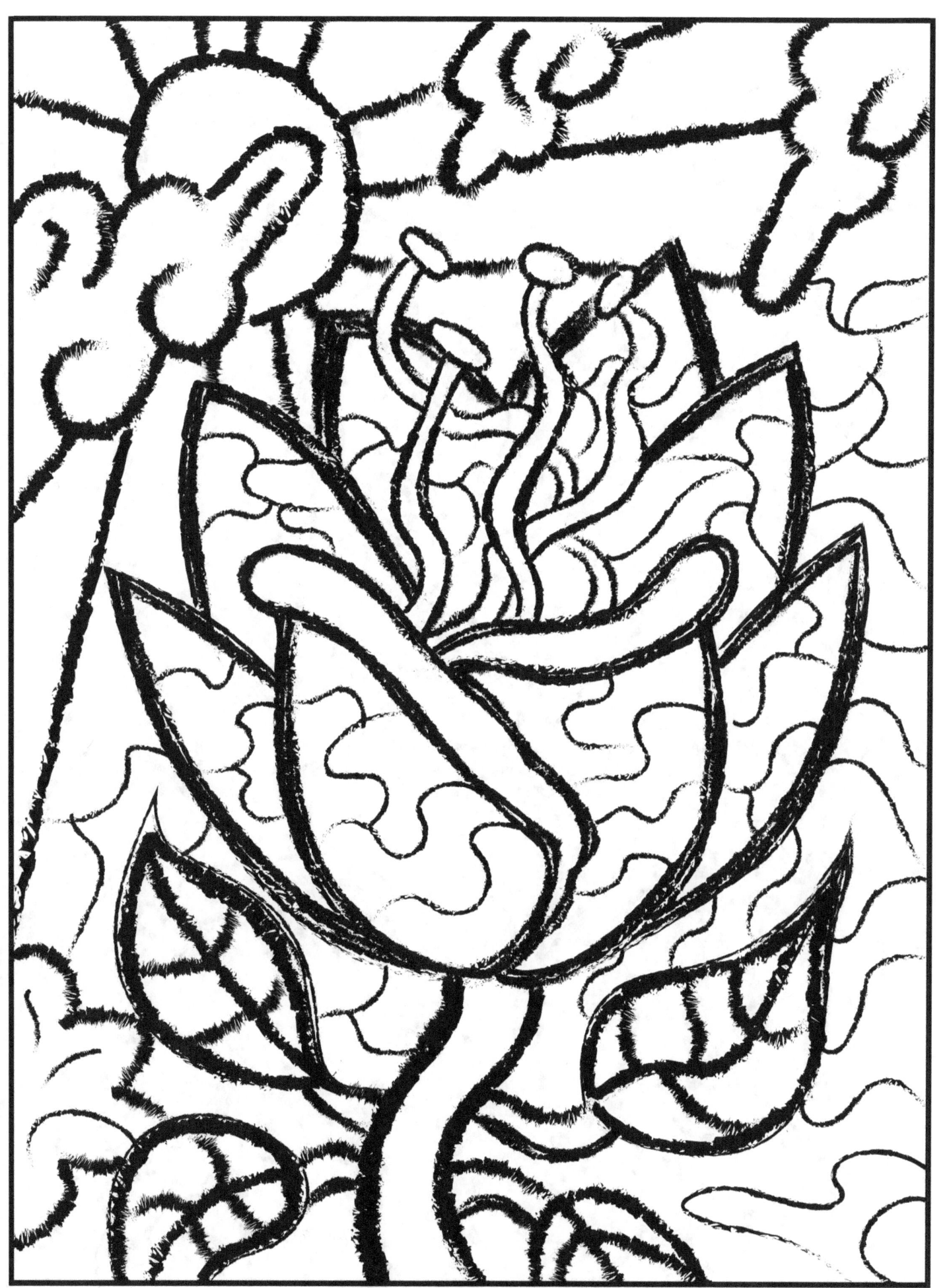

JOHNSPAINART.COM - DYNAMIC IMAGINATION

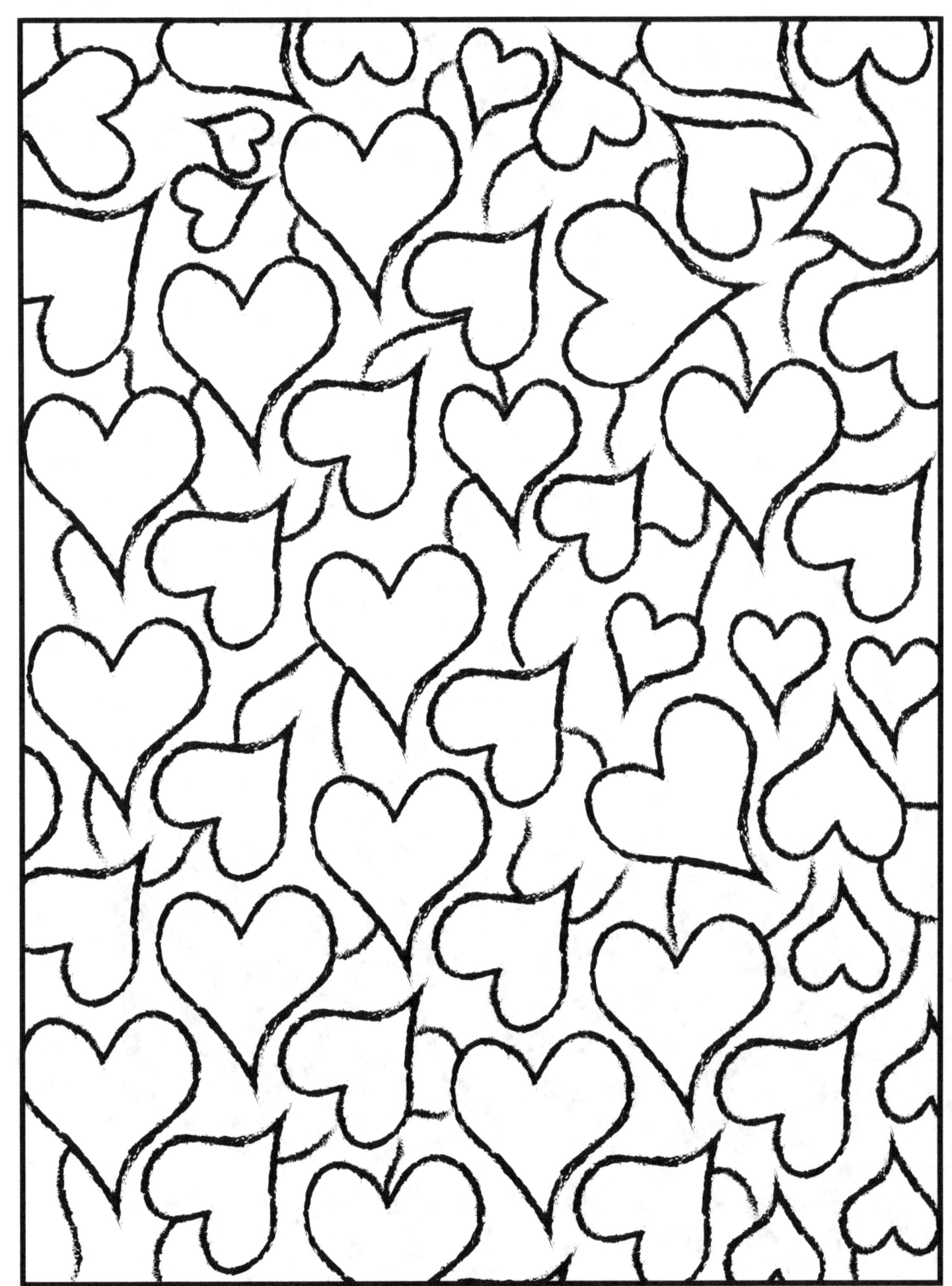

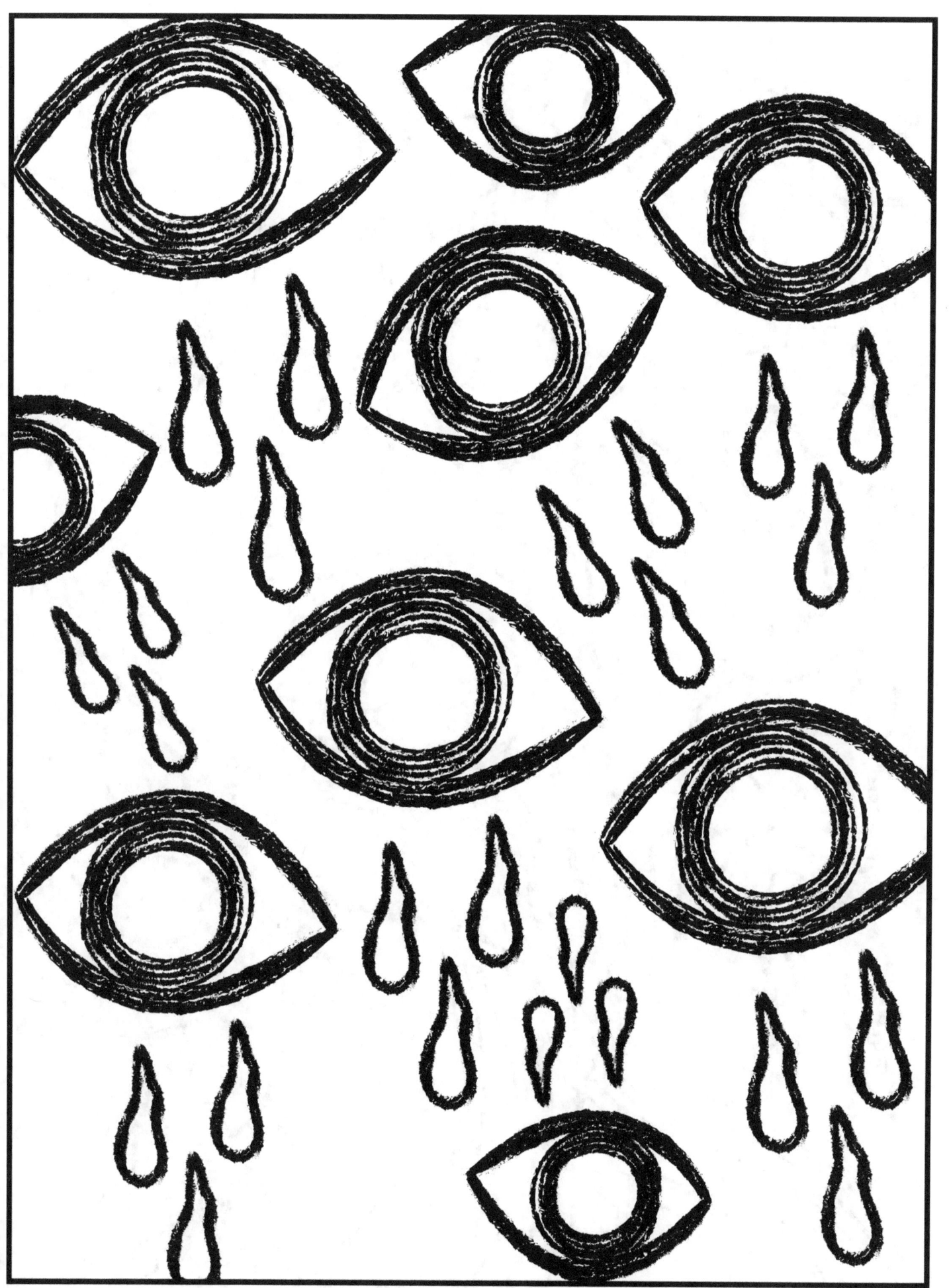

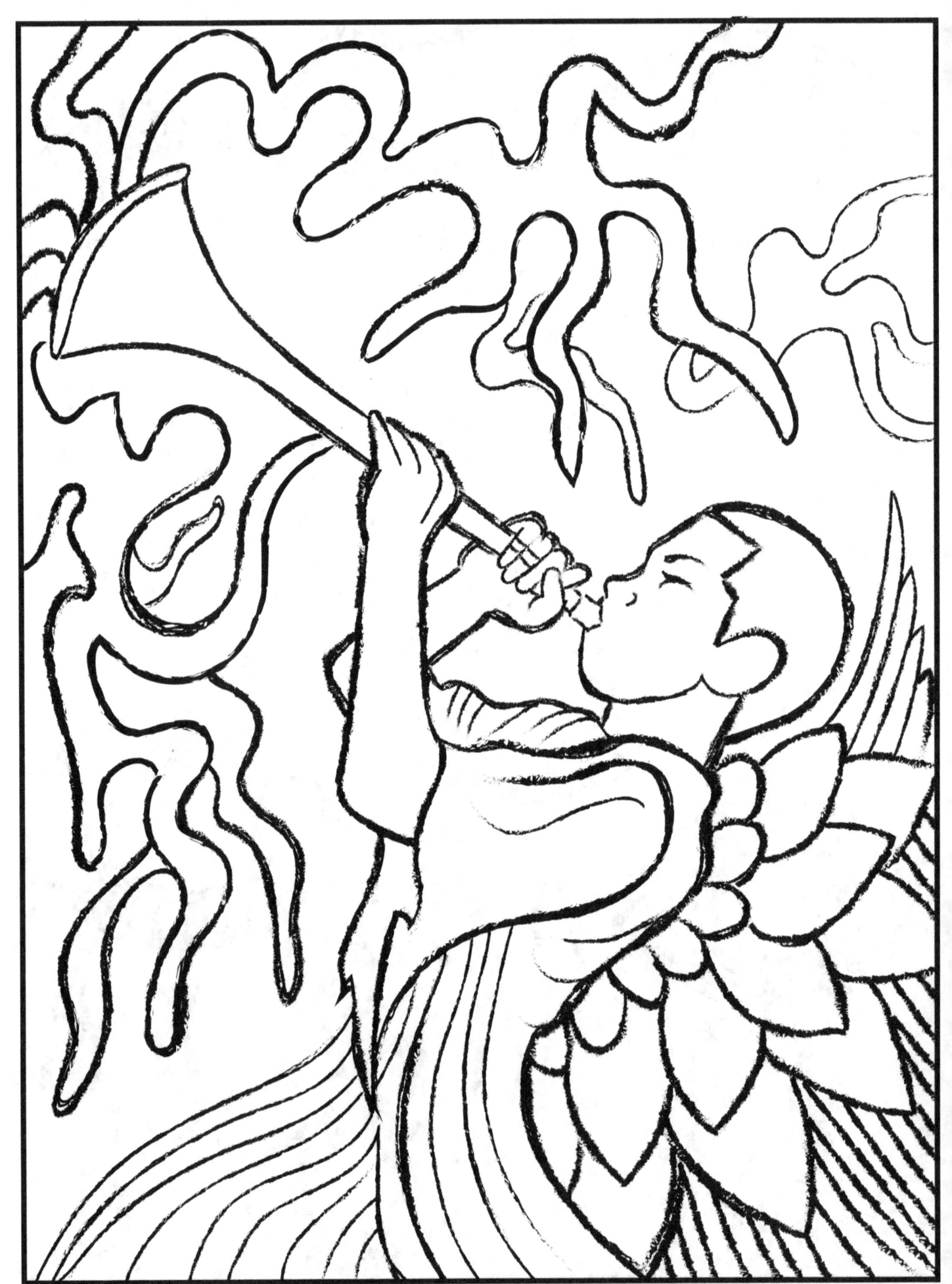

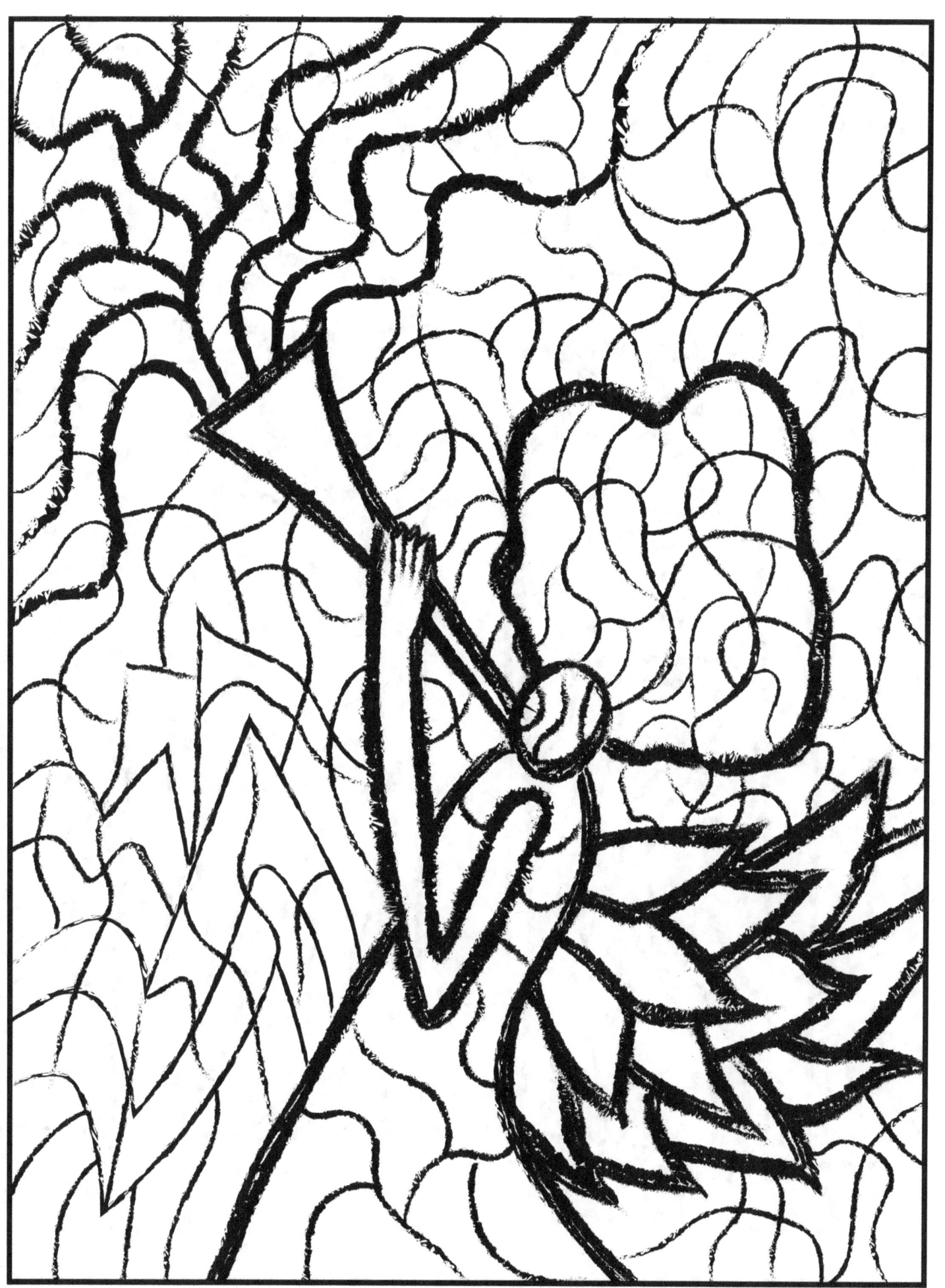

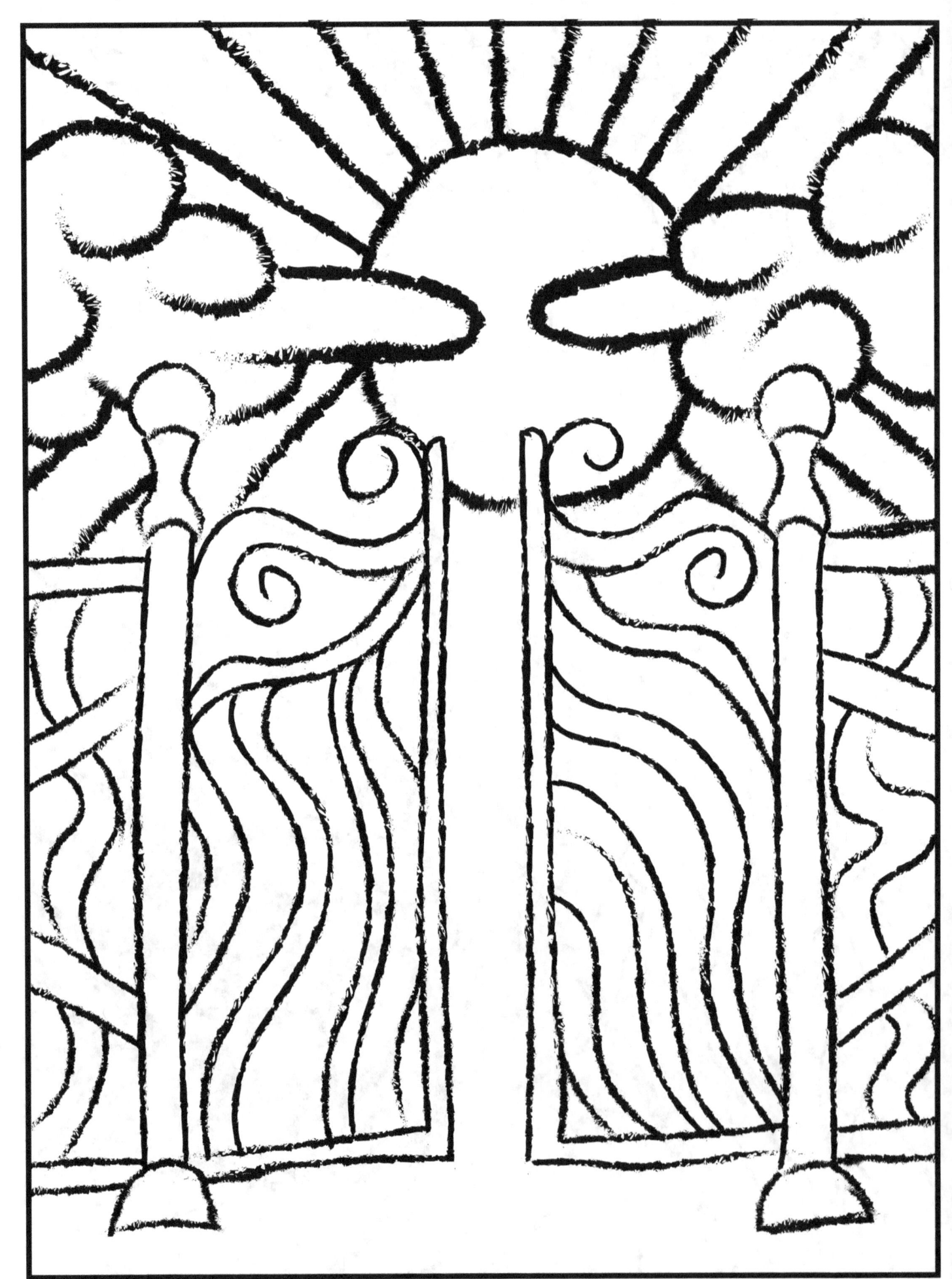